I Made It

Meiner lieben Freundin
Ursiela zum Andenken.
Weihnachten 2011.
Sigrid.

I Made It

A Story About Youth and
War and Immigration

Sigrid B. Josam

Library of Congress Control Number: 2011919295
ISBN: Hardcover   978-1-4653-8796-7
                  Softcover   978-1-4653-8795-0
                  Ebook   978-1-4653-8797-4

This book was printed in the United States of America.

To order additional copies of this book, contact:
Xlibris Corporation
1-888-795-4274
www.Xlibris.com
Orders@Xlibris.com
103849

CONTENTS

PREFACE

I want to thank Professor Rick Lott at Arkansas State University in Jonesboro for encouraging me to write my story. I also thank my Sunday school teacher, Catherine Edgar, Eula Schell, and Alice Bryant for weeding out my spelling mistakes and helping with the computer. I wrote this book for my children, grandchildren, great-grandchildren, and all future generations. Maybe it will discourage people from waging war.

My story may not have all the correct dates, but that is not important. The names have been changed. The way a child feels and the things we have to do just to stay alive are what's important. I hope that other young people will read this and realize that life could be a lot worse and that it is important to study our history and language as well as other countries' history and language. Personal visits to other countries will lead to better understanding. Maybe later, I will write about my life in the United States. The first years were not easy, but we made it. I am proud of what we accomplished and how my children and grandchildren are doing. I hope and wish that no one has to go through a war in their own country like we had ever again. Visiting military museums is still very hard for me. I cannot tolerate more than five airplanes above, movies with lots of shooting, and searchlights that point at the sky. I completely understand when our soldiers return from a war and they have problems integrate themselves back into society. They have seen things that are impossible to forget, and it changes one's life.

I like to share a poem with you about something that is constantly on my mind. This is a beautiful country, and we have to take care of it.

Do something!

Count your blessing, take care of the land.
Dont build houses on shifting sand.
Be it the mountains or the sea,
Built for the future four our children to see.
Many lives were lost when we fought for this land.
Get involved, take a stand.

I MADE IT

My life may sound hard to many who are reading this, but since I knew no other way, it seemed okay for me for a long time. There were also lots of happy moments, though I always knew that I wanted to change things as I grew up. Sure, we were poor people, and I lived through World War II under American, Russian, and British occupation. It was also scary to live under Hitler's regime.

But let me start on March 7, 1930, the day I was born. My father was not home when labor started, and Mom had to walk the thirty minutes to the hospital alone. A policeman accompanied her when he saw her on the street. My father was playing cards and drinking beer with his buddies in a pub. After Mom had been in the hospital for two days, my father went to see her but only after his friend had asked for Mom and told him to go to the hospital where she could probably be. He was very disappointed that I was a girl. The seventh had been a busy day; twelve boys were born that day, and I was the only girl. Since they had only twelve baby beds, I was put into a bed with a little boy. His name was Ralf, and his mother became Mom's friend. She also arranged for my parents to move into the same apartment. It was still the Depression, and apartments were hard to find at a reasonable price.

We moved into a one-bedroom apartment that had a living room and kitchen. The living room was only used in winter and on Sundays and holidays. The entrance to our apartment was quite large, like a normal room; we used that as a playroom. These are some of the things Mom told me as I pushed her in a wheelchair through the park before her death. We would spend hours talking about times past. How sad it is to have a father who cared so little about his wife and about his daughter. I felt so sorry for Mom to have had a life like that.

My first memories go back to the time when I was three years old. I had measles. It was before Christmas, and after I felt better, I begged Mom to take me to the grocery store with her. I remember how she bundled me up in a light-gray winter coat. December is a very cold month in Germany, with either snow or rain and cold winds. I did get sick again after that short outing. The doctor came twice a week to look after me, but I did not improve. Day and night, I had to sleep on the living room sofa, where it was warmer. Mom kept the oven going twenty-four hours a day. After being sick for several weeks at home, the doctor put me in the hospital. My parents were told that I would not live much longer. At the time, I had double pneumonia, double pleurisy, and some other ailments I don't remember. I remember the nurse taking my temperature, and I remember myself always crying till the nurse pointed at the other little boy in my room and said, "Look at that little boy, he does not cry when his temperature is taken." I was very much ashamed and would behave after that. The nurses wore long dark uniforms and little starched white caps; I felt intimidated just looking at them, especially since I had never seen anyone dressed like that before.

Tears flowed when I caught a glimpse of my mom looking through the glass door and the nurse bringing me my doll. That meant Mom had come, but she was not allowed in my room. She was pregnant with my sister at the time. I don't think anyone explained that to me. I felt abandoned and scared being in the hospital, and not seeing Mom made it a lot worse. I remember waking up in a dark room, lying on a gurney. Only a candle was burning in a far corner of the room. There were no windows in the room, only that candle spread some light. I cried till someone took me out of that room. Had I died, or was I close to it? Another time, I was put in a bed with all my clothes on. Also, my winter coat and a heavy feather bed were put on top of me. The nurse pushed my bed toward an open window on the ground floor. It was a sunny day in February, and my parents, along with Mom's brother and his wife, were staying outside.

Geranium pots were arranged on the windowsill, which Mom pushed aside. I jumped up in bed, and we briefly hugged. The nurse had turned her back for a moment while we were embracing. I presume today that I needed an oxygen tank, which had not been invented then. Slowly my health improved, and a nurse took me for a stroll around the park in an old-fashioned baby carriage. Every hospital in Germany had a park with benches where people could leisurely walk or sit down once they began to feel better. Patients stayed in the hospital longer those days. It was nice to get outside in the fresh spring air. The trees had already a light shade of green, a promise that the leaves would come out soon. Crocuses were blooming, and the tops of daffodils were breaking through the ground.

On my birthday, I was permitted to get out of bed and Mom could visit. We sat at a little children's table across a little boy who was also celebrating his birthday. His mother had brought bananas, my favorite fruit. His mother gave me one too, which made me very happy. Bananas are still my favorite fruit today. Again, I had to wear a borrowed dress, which was too large, and the house shoes made from camel hair slipped easily off my feet.

My hospital stay was six weeks. Before I was released, I was put into a room with six other girls. At bedtime, I was told to stay in my crib. The other children were older and chased each other around the room after the nurse turned off the lights. Up and down on the beds, around and around the room. They did not hear my plea to get my potty, and since the nurse had told me not to get up, I wet the bed. When the nurse checked on us later, she was very disappointed, which made me feel real sad. I learned that one does not always have to follow instructions exactly; rules can and have to be changed according to the circumstances. I could have pulled the bell string to call the nurse, but then the other kids would have been mad at me for interrupting their playtime. Mom had told me it was wrong to tell on people, so I had kept quiet, I did not defend myself.

After six weeks, I was allowed to go home. I must have been too weak to walk because we took a taxi, which was really too expensive for my family. When I arrived home, all the children in our apartment house were waiting to greet me, but looking back, they were probably attracted to the taxi, an unlikely happening in our neighborhood.

My sister, Renate, was born on May 4, 1934. Mom left me with her uncle while she was away in the hospital. Uncle Herman and Aunt Hermine were nice, soft-spoken people. Their son was nice too but more boisterous; he was my age. We used to visit them once in a while. Their apartment was larger, and they had a big garden with lots of fruit trees and berry bushes, also flowers and vegetables in abundance. It was a place where I could get my hands dirty digging in the soil. The garden also had a small cabin, which looked so pretty in the middle of all the greenery. When it was time to go home, we would always get a large bag filled with all kinds of fruits and vegetables.

It was asparagus time when I stayed with them. The region around Brunswick (Braunschweig), my hometown, is famous for its white asparagus. The sandy soil is perfect for growing the white variety. Aunt Hermine grew some in her own garden, and she would serve asparagus twice weekly. I love asparagus now, but it was my least favorite vegetable at that time. That is all I remember from that visit, sitting at the kitchen table and trying to eat some of those white stalks. It always took a long time before I was finished with my supper. I remember Aunt Hermine always wearing a housedress or an apron, standing at the stove in the kitchen, stirring and cooking something. Her brown hair was arranged in a bun in the back of her neck. I always thought that she looked more like a grandmother. The bedroom I was sleeping in had a very large chest standing against one wall. I imagined all kinds of scary things that might be in there. Since it was so long, I thought that a person could be hiding in there. At bedtime, I would always eye it suspiciously.

I was relieved when Mom finally came to get me. Now I could see my little baby sister. She was so tiny, only six pounds; I had been a ten-pound baby. It was easy to make her smile; I made all kinds of funny faces at her. That ability to laugh together carried over later in our life. We could start laughing at any time over the silliest things and had a hard time stopping. It felt good to be silly when we were adults.

Our living room door had a window on top, and when Renate was in her baby bed, we could just look through the window to see if Renate was all right. Mom had moved her bed close to the wall, and as soon as Renate could sit up, she kept herself busy peeling the wallpaper off the wall. Her tiny fingers could dig into the paper and tear tiny long strips out. Mom made the mistake of just moving the bed, and the next day, more strips were hanging down the wall. After that we moved her bed more to the middle of the room. As soon as Mom had some extra money, she purchased some wallpaper. She could not get the same pattern anymore and had to take something similar just for the bottom part of the wall. We had to live with that for a long time, way after the war was over.

Every year, Renate would get chocolate *Maikaefer*, or May beetles, or cockchafers as they are called here, for her birthday. For each year she had lived, one of those chocolate beetles would grace the table. They were wrapped in shiny golden paper. On her fourth birthday, four of them graced the table. It was especially quiet in the living room, and as I looked through the window, I saw how she bit off the end of each bug and folded the paper neatly over its tail again. When she was four, she was the size of a two-year-old. How she managed to climb up that chair to reach the tabletop is a mystery. We used to play lots of games, and Renate won most of them. When we went to the West Coast in 1986 and gambled some in Las Vegas, she won too. After I started school, I read all of our children's books to her. We had no radio, so reading was a wonderful diversion. I still remember some chapters of our books today. Those things are still in my head, but other more recent happenings, I forgot.

Our parents divorced when I was five years old. My father had hit my mother in one of his drunken stupors. I heard the commotion and was very frightened by it. Seeing my mother in tears always made me cry too. I never really missed my father; he never took us into his arms. All I remembered were his spankings and arguments with my mother. He always demanded something special for dinner. He would get the larger steak or the longest sausage. He would never share his meal with us. Many years later, when we went to Germany for a visit, his grandsons could have his meat. At the time, he could be generous, and he was proud of them and of me that I had given birth to two sons.

As children, we would collect May beetles, which were plentiful and destructive. Early morning was the best time to collect them when the bugs were still sluggish. We punctured the lids of shoe cartons, lined the inside with some leaves, and started to collect them. Sometimes we shook the smaller trees, and the bugs fell to the ground. Our cartons filled up pretty fast. The bugs had different markings on their backs, and we named them Miller, Baker, Chimneysweep, and many other names I can't recall. The boys loved to chase us girls, trying to set the bugs in our hair or on our arms, which I disliked very much. I hated it when they dug into our skin and crawled up our arms. They were a plague then in our region but are mostly extinct now. In other parts of Germany, they are coming back and are destructive again. They can eat the leaves of a tree in one day. I preferred the chocolate ones with the golden paper wrapping.

Next to our house was a storage space for an appliance store. The stoves were packed in wet excelsior, which protected them from damage when they were moved. Every month, someone would come and take some appliances back to the store. This was an opportunity for us children to go there and play hide-and-seek in the hollowed spaces. We were always at least six children playing. The man who picked up the ovens did not mind.

On one of those days, he came into my hiding place with me. I was not alarmed since he had gone with the other children into their hiding places before too. When he touched me inappropriately, I got scared. He told me not to tell anyone, but I ran home quickly and told Mom. She looked very upset and went to the police. As soon as the children in our house were notified to appear in court as witnesses, the torture began for me. The children made fun of me and called me names. We could tell exactly what was talked about around their dinner table at home. They repeated what their parents had said. I was often in tears, but Mom would say I had to be strong and it would pass. I'm sure that man had done the same to the other children; they just had not told their parents.

It took some time after the trial before life returned to normal. The trial was the worst thing. The courthouse was already intimidating. It was a large building with long floors to the courtrooms. The doors seemed triple the size of our doors at home. Then all these strange men were asking me all these questions, asking where I was touched when I didn't know the names of my body parts. Nobody talked about those things in 1935, at least not in my family. The man was sentenced to one year in jail.

I had just turned six when school started. On the first day of school, German children carry a *Schultuete*, a cone-shaped bag, about twenty inches high. Mine was a bright-red color with a picture of a blond girl in front. Inside the bag were some chocolate candy, a bright-yellow ball with red and blue dots, and a fancy handkerchief. This custom started in 1817, and they still have it today. If you ever have a chance to go to Germany in the fall when the new school year starts, you can see the *Schultueten* in every store where school supplies are sold. It certainly sweetens the first day of school. And just recently, I read in a magazine that this custom will come to the United States too.

SCHULTUETE

When I started school, the school year started in spring. Several years later, it was changed to fall. My first-grade teacher was a young man; we all loved him. He made learning interesting, and he was fair. He also taught us how to play the recorder. The first year, we also had a school fest. We dressed in our Sunday best and played games.

Whoever won got a prize, and later, a cake and a hot chocolate were served. I remember only the first fest. I was wearing this beautiful light-blue silk dress and a wreath with little white flowers in my hair. We went to this restaurant only on special occasions, like the time when Oma came for a visit. *Oma* is the short version of *Grossmutter* or grandmother in German. *Opa* is the German word for grandfather. She enjoyed the trapeze performance right over our heads, the performance of the comedians and other artists on the stage. It was fun for us to see her face and hear her exclamations. It was something special for her. She was always so busy on her little farm; here she had a special week with us.

Once a year, the kids in the city schools were sent to an estate in the country for two weeks to get fresh country air. Not every family was financially able to go on vacation in the summer. The children with parents who had a limited income paid only ten or twenty marks for those two weeks; I don't remember. Three classes of different grades were going at the same time. The older children would help in the dining room, cleaning the tables, and maybe picking vegetables for the day in its large garden. Herr Kutter, our teacher, would come in the morning, still in his pajamas, playing a song on the recorder to awaken us. At bedtime, he had a piece of candy for every child. Not such a good idea eating candy after we had brushed our teeth, but some of us felt homesick at first. We were not used to sleepovers as children are today. For most of us, it was the first time away from home. The candy distracted us, and getting it before bedtime made it even more special. At least six of us slept in a room, and other rooms had eight to twelve beds. Our classrooms had between forty to fifty children, with boys and girls in separate classes.

After awakening in the morning, we dressed in our gym clothes and met in the park for gymnastics. To clean up, we had to use the large basins in the washroom. Each basin had about eight faucets. We had to undress in there and wash ourselves, which was embarrassing at first. But we all got used to it pretty fast; besides, by then we were hungry and anxious to get breakfast. Later, we made our beds and then had two hours of schooling three times a week. After class we marched, three in a row, into the woods. We learned about the plants and insects till we went back to the estate, always singing. I still remember those songs. Later, when I was already living in the United States, I would include some rhymes and texts in the letters when I wrote home. It inspired Mom to test me, Renate, and herself too to see how much each of us remembered. The winner would get a silver spoon from her. Guess who won? It was I who got the spoon. After lunch, we had to rest for an hour, and the whole afternoon belonged to us to do what we liked. That wonderful large park was so inviting, those very old trees giving shade during the day. The hedges around the park were great hiding places to read or play with our dolls. No one would disturb us. We had jumping ropes and balls to play games till suppertime. After supper, our teacher would read a story to us, and at 8:00 PM, it was time for bed.

I have wonderful memories, except for one year when some of the kids got diphtheria. The sickroom filled up pretty quick. We could not go home after the usual two weeks and had to stay two weeks longer to avoid infecting the children at home. The doctor diagnosed a heart problem when I fainted one day. I had to stay in bed for three days and was permitted to go out again after that. Our doctor at home could not find anything wrong with my heart when we got back. But I fainted often as a child after that episode and could never stay still in one place at any length of time. Just like now, it is still the same; but now I remember to sit down when feeling dizzy.

Back home, I got hurt when one of the boys tried to throw a brick over a wall, except the brick did not go over the wall; it landed right on my head. We kids had been watching with fascination as the brick did not make it. I wish I had been smart enough to run away, but it all happened so fast. I was screaming when I saw all the blood on my hands and felt it running down my face. The manager of the electric store in our house just came out of the store and quickly drove my mother and me to the doctor in his gray Mercedes. Mom wound a towel around my head to save his upholstery from blood splatters. It did not feel good when the doctor cleaned the wound; it felt like a brush was swirled around the hole in my head.

Ralf, who had thrown the brick, was really a nice guy and had never been in trouble before. He is also the one I had shared the bed with in the hospital; I think we shared a special bond. We were friends for many years. His mother broke three umbrellas on his backsides for throwing the brick. Those were the years when parents believed that spanking would take care of everything. My mom would do the same when we had misbehaved. One time I got a spanking just for asking if one of the ladies in our house had her baby yet. I was already ten years old. As little as I was, I made up my mind not to overreact to simple questions when I had children. Another time I told the son of a friend of ours that babies grew under a mother's heart. Mom had told me, and I related the answer to him. His mother had just had a baby girl, and he was confused. When his mother found out what I had done, she called Mom, and I received a severe spanking. Mom also wrote a letter to a home for troubled children. That letter was never mailed; Mom kept it in her desk for many years. I checked often to see if it was still there. Did she think that letter would keep me in line? It would have brought us so much closer if she had answered my questions. We children see and hear things, and we need some answers. Nothing explicit, just general information. But Mom grew up with stepmothers, and they did not talk about those things to her either.

The children in our house usually played well together. But with twenty children, disagreements do happen. I would forgive them several times when they bothered me before I acted; but if the teasing and pushing would not stop, I reacted. I was not scared to beat anybody up. One boy who lived a block away had not stopped bothering me after several warnings. He was shorter than me but strong. When he noticed my upraised arms, he ran away. I knew he was a fast runner and he was counting on that, but so was I. It took me the whole block to catch up with him right on his front door. I threw him on the ground and started hitting him. Since I was afraid he might get up, I sat on his back and then got scared that after I got up, he would come after me. I was out of breath from the long run, and my arms were shaking; they were tired from hitting him. Nothing happened when I got up; he ran crying upstairs to his mother, and I could slowly walk back home. He never bothered me again. It also impressed the other children, and I was left in peace.

Reading books was my favorite pastime when I was young. Friends would lend them to me. My favorites were *Heidi, Nora* and the Nesthäkchen books by Else Ury. She was a Jewish author who lived in Switzerland; her books were later forbidden by the Hitler regime. Most people would not obey the new law to burn her books. Else wrote ten Nesthäkchen books, I believe. I would read them again today if I could find them. *Nesthäkchen* means the youngest child in the family. It told about the life of a young girl growing up until she got married. Reading those books would transfer me into another world, make me wish for a whole family. As I write this book, I finally discovered a place where I can order her books in German, but only in paperback, and I did. Reading them again was a nice experience, reliving the days of my youth. I was also a steady customer at the library. I could forget everything around me when reading, which happened quite often. Mom had three jobs after the divorce, so I had to watch my little sister all the time.

I had to prepare simple meals at times, which was not so bad; but Renate had her own ideas on what to do and when. Many times she would just sneak out of the door and play somewhere without telling me. And my imagination would run away with me; I worried and cried till I found her. Mom could have gone on welfare, but she was too proud. So we were alone a lot, and when Renate disappeared, I would get mad and give her a spanking when I finally found her. She would tell Mom after she came home from work, and we both got a spanking—Renate for running away and I for spanking her.

In winter, we would go sledding. We had a pretty steep hill in a park close by. The police did not want us to do this. Our sleds would run all the way to the sidewalks, endangering the pedestrians. We were always on the lookout for police and ran away when they came in sight. Everyone would holler "Police, police!" and we would run away in all directions as fast as we could, only to come back as soon as the coast was clear again. The sleds would be confiscated if we had been caught and taken to the police station, where a parent had to pick them up. One time, my sled ran into a tree. My back hurt so much that I could not walk, and the kids in our house had to pull me home on the sled. When Mom came home from work that evening, I was a lot better and did not tell her of my mishap. Another spanking besides the back pain would have been too much.

Birthdays and Christmases were special. I could invite my friends to my birthdays. Mom would bake a cake, which was always a lot of fun. I held on to the bowl while she stirred the dough. Slowly, when one or two of my fingers would slide over the rim of the bowl to catch some of the dough, I would see a grin on Mom's face. We could also lick the stirring spoon clean. She would leave some dough on there while Renate and I watched each other carefully that neither would get more than the other. After drinking hot chocolate and eating cake, we played games. Later, Mom would serve Jell-O pudding. The rule was, whoever spilled some of the wobbly pudding would get a spanking. Those were not real spankings, just a little slap on our behind, nothing painful. With a bunch of girls giggling and eating that wobbly pudding, it would get spilled eventually by someone. Before everybody went home, there was *Topfklopfen.* An old cooking pot was turned around and a present put under it. Each girl took turns getting her eyes covered with a scarf and had a walking cane put in her hand. She would try to find the pot and take the present. The walking canes were made out of wood; my parents used them on outings to the Harz Mountains, one hour's train ride away from Brunswick. The front of the walking cane had metal pictures from different cities one had visited over the years. Mine has seventeen metal plates with the pictures all down the front and back. I still have mine today; I saved it all these years. For one of my birthdays, I got a chocolate handbag, wrapped in silvery paper with a real handle. I thought that was the prettiest present ever. For two years I looked at it, stroked it often, and smiled. When I finally decided to eat it, the chocolate was gray inside, so we had to throw it away. I still remember the emotion I felt when my hand had to let go of it.

Roller-skating was one of my favorite pastimes, and I was quite good at it. We only had one pair of skates, which Renate and I had to share. Since they were not attached to boots, we had to change the length of the skates all the time. The other ones were too expensive for us. We did not have skating rinks then like you have here. Our skates had to be clamped on to our shoe soles and would eventually cause the soles to come loose—a bad thing to happen since we could only get one new pair of shoes a year during the war. The shoe repairman would attach little metal disks on the front of our soles and on the back of the heels. The undersole would get metal pins that looked a lot like upholstery pins. It made a lot of noise when walking, but the soles and heels lasted a lot longer this way since we walked everywhere. No school buses, no parents who would drive children to school. Summer or winter, rain or sleet, we walked to school. We used umbrellas and rubber boots. Our raincoats would hang outside the classroom, and the boots would stand there in a row, drying till we went home again.

It must have been 1934 or 1935 when my father had to join the Nazi Party. I remember that he had to march on the streets during evening hours and came home very tired. His boss had been threatened that his shop would be closed if his employees would not join the party. It was still the Depression, and the men needed the jobs to feed their families; so they did not complain, they endured.

The summer of 1938 found my sister and me going by train to visit our grandparents in Thuringia. It was an eight-hour train ride. We had a name tag around our neck with the train ticket inside. A nurse would meet us at each train change (we had to make three) and bring us to the connecting train. It takes about four hours by car today, but the trains had to go around the mountains, making the trip longer. Thuringia is called the green heart of Germany. It's mountainous with villages and cities embedded in the valleys—very picturesque, especially in the spring when all the fruit trees are blooming. We left our hometown with the usual instructions: "Don't talk to strangers, don't accept food from anyone. Wash your hands before you eat and after you finished, and be good." I had a little pouch for a wet washcloth and did as Mom had instructed us. Not so with Renate, she did as she pleased. As the nurse accompanied us to the connecting train, she offered us peppermint candy. I said, "No, thank you," but Renate happily munched the candy in front of me, avoiding my accusing glances. After our last train change, a lady from Grandma's village entered the car with a large basket of cherries. She offered us some; and since I remembered her from former visits, I politely took a handful, went to the open window, and dropped all of them out. Renate ate all of hers. Mom had told me not to take anything from strangers; it really hurt sometimes to follow her advice.

My worried grandmother had waited for the first train in the morning even when we had not left our hometown. She was so afraid that she would miss us. It was unheard of in that village that two small children, ages eight and four, would make that eight-hour trip alone. Oma came to the railroad station with a handcart for our suitcase. Renate had to be put in the cart too; her little legs got tired on the long way to Oma's house. Grandfather, or Opa, was all smiles when he saw us; but his handlebar mustache was scratchy when we gave him a kiss. He would get only two kisses: one when we arrived and the other when we left and said good-bye.

My father's older sister, Irma, had been visiting and left about the time we arrived. She cried when she kissed her mother good-bye. That was all I needed to get homesick and start crying. Renate missed me and called my name, "Sigrid, where are you?" I had disappeared into the outside toilet. Renate started crying too when she saw my tears. But it did not last long; we soon went out to look around the house, the garden, and the barn. There was always so much to see and do at Grandma's.

Our bedroom was on the second floor. Our beds had straw mattresses on the bottom with huge feather beds on top, you could cuddle into at night. When I stood up in bed, I could almost touch the ceiling. I tried to do that every year when we visited, but it took several years more before I could accomplish that task. Two large wardrobes were in our room. One was filled with linens. Oma still had new linens from the time she got married. Every hand towel, dish towel, and every tablecloth had her hand-embroidered initials in them. Sheets and pillowcases also. I loved to look at those treasures. I would do the same later in my life before I got married. We learned the stitching in school. I had to embroider the initials from our school in the principal's towels too. But Oma's stitching was a lot better than mine. I have some of her towels now and would not know how to copy her work.

The other wardrobe held Oma's special clothes, which consisted of dresses for weddings and funerals. The clothes were handmade and decorated with lots of tiny pleats in the front. She had done beautiful work. Little hats or caps embroidered with tiny pearls came with each outfit. I loved to look at them all. She had done this on winter nights before she got married. The single girls would meet during the week and sew their outfits by hand. Had I inherited some of her talent? I had been clothes conscious at three; is there a connection? She would also wear capes over her dresses in the winter. The cape had a large collar that would reach all the way to her waist. The purpose was to wrap your babies in there while holding them in your arms. It was easier to carry a child that way; the children would not feel as heavy and at the same time were protected from the cold. She had those capes in cotton fabrics for the summer and a Sunday dress for summer and winter. Opa's clothes were not as interesting for me. But he had the special clothes from years back, which were worn only on special occasions. Our bedroom had white cotton curtains on the windows, dressed up with handmade lace. And since the windows were kept open most of the time in the summer months, every room had long sticky flycatchers hanging from the ceiling.

It was fun to watch our grandparents milk the cows and feed the calfs, swines, goats, and chickens. Sometimes we had ducks too. Every room in the house, including the pigsty, cowshed, and barn had a bundle of herbs hanging from a corner on the ceiling. They were there to protect the house from evil spirits, just in case. Everybody had rabbits; they multiplied so fast that we had one for Sunday dinner several times during the year. We made hay, which took several hot sunny days to get dry enough to bring home, and stored it in the barn. Hay was made in the summer and early fall. In between the grass was cut and fed fresh to the animals. The fresh grass yielded more milk from the cows and goats. The grass had to be cut on a hot, dry summer day. Opa loaded the wagon, and we children could sit on top of the load on the way home.

When it was time to do the laundry, Oma would boil the white linen and cotton clothes in her large copper tub in the kitchen. That tub was also used for making syrup from sugar beets and marmalade from prunes. Aunt Lora, my father's younger sister, would help her. Instead of hanging the clothes up to dry, we laid them in the grassy yard across the street. As soon as they had dried, I would take a sprinkling can and wet them. The water would come out of an old hand pump, which stood in the garden. I had to repeat this several times during the day. The results were perfectly white clothes, bleached by the sun, and with no chemicals. If you think, *What about the bugs?* Don't worry. There are not as many as we have here; it depends a lot on the climate. I liked that old pump. It was different from what we had seen before. You had to pour some water in the pump first before the constant pumping of the handle would suction up the water.

We helped or stood in the way when the grain was cut, bundled, dried, and threshed. Later, when I was thirteen years old, I could load the wagon with the bundles of wheat. A large beam attached to chains held the high load of grain down. Opa never said it, but I could tell by his smile that he was proud of me.

I also had my first boyfriend that year. His grandmother's house was next to my grandparents' house. He would sit on her porch and play the same songs on his accordion as I did on the recorder on our side. There was a wall between us; we did not see each other playing our instruments. A bunch of us children would also go in the woods and pick berries. It started when the wild strawberries ripened; and after a while, the blueberries ripened, then the raspberries, elderberries, and blackberries. We drank elderberry juice to prevent colds, which I still do today. Before our vacation came to an end, the cow calved. We had strict instructions to stay inside, but you guessed it, Renate did not listen. She slipped into the cowshed and held on to one of the neighbors' boots and watched as the calf was pulled out. None of the people complained; everyone just laughed, and I felt like a fool staying inside the house.

When Mom picked us up at the railroad station and we were on our way home in the tramcar, Renate's heart was overflowing with joy. She could not wait till we got home. She entertained all the people with her story on how the cow had calved. One lady enjoyed it so much that she gave Renate a whole bar of chocolate. I did not get anything even though I had behaved and not spoken out loud. Life was not fair sometimes. This would happen to me all the time, and I would complain to Mom many times that she favored my sister. She always denied this. I wanted some hugging too; she would always say, "You are too big or too old for something like that." I was only four years older than Renate. Many years later, when Mom was in her seventies and faced gallbladder surgery, a letter came in which she apologized for having favored my sister. At that time in her life, she wanted to clear her conscience. It did make me feel better; I also was old enough by then to have forgiven her. But when we got home from our vacation, all our dolls had flowers in their hands and a placard that said Welcome Home. She had also invited our friends the next day for hot chocolate and doughnuts, which we called *Berliner Pfannkuchen* in Germany.

It was 1939 when I found my mother crying, sitting on the couch in the kitchen. When I asked her why, she said, "You won't understand, war broke out." I did not understand; I had no idea what was awaiting us, what could and would happen. Soon our lives would change drastically. It started with putting black window shades on every window in our apartment. The automobile lights were covered so that only small slits of light would show. This was done so the enemy bombers would not see the cities below; it was for our safety. The same precautions had to be made with the headlights on our bicycles and the street lanterns. The streets became very dark at night especially in the winter months. Many times on a cloudy night, people would collide with other pedestrians when they came home from work. I don't remember car accidents. After a while, only businesspeople and the very rich had cars. Cars were confiscated, used for the war effort. People colliding did not happen as often after the glowing coat pins became available. You could tell if someone was approaching. Mom's pin was a schnauzer, a pin of a dog. During the summer months, we had no problems colliding at night; it stayed light outside till ten thirty at night. Then ration cards were issued for food and clothing. Radios with amplifiers were on street corners announcing the winnings at first. People stood and listened. I was only nine years old, but I disliked Hitler's powerful voice. I was drawn to it and repelled by it at the same time. It frightened me and made me run home faster. Caught listening to the BBC would mean punishment with doing civic duty like cleaning the streets of debris after a bombing.

Telling political jokes was also punished with jail. I had listened at the door one time when we had company. The joke my mother told our friends was political. We children were sent to bed first, which made me think this would be interesting. I sneaked out of bed and listened at the door. The children of Goering and Goebbels were walking around a potty with lighted candles in their hands. Goering asked, "What are you doing?" The children answered, "You make a torch parade over every little piece of shit too." The joke weighed heavily on my mind all through the war. As much as I wanted to tell my friends, I did not dare; it could have meant jail for Mom if someone had told the authorities. This joke I still remember, and all the others I heard over my lifetime are forgotten. This also cured me of being nosy; never again would I listen through a door.

My mother's sister, Aunt Luise, had come to our city from the French border with her husband, Andreas. They told us that the French people had mined our coal mines from the French side. Aunt Luise's home was damaged by the first bombing in my hometown. It was an awful sound when the alarm started. In the beginning, most people would not go to the air-raid shelters. Many times the planes just flew over our city and dropped the bombs some other place. We could see the silvery vapor trails of the so tiny-looking planes high up in the sky during the day. When the first bombs fell, it all changed very fast. Before we could get dressed, the bombs were falling and our machine guns were shooting back. The noise was awful, and the shrapnel was flying around us as we ran for cover. It was a miracle that we made it safely into the shelter.

People came hastily dressed; children were tired, pulled out of their sleep crying. Half the people had part of their clothes hanging over their handbags. Maybe I have to explain why people came into the shelters like that. It was the more-endowed women who had bras and girdles to hold their stockings up with lots of hooks for closures. It would take them a lot longer to get dressed; those undergarments were expensive. You had to make a choice: die correctly dressed or be safely in the shelter alive.

But it surely looked funny seeing those items hanging loosely over the pocketbooks of the ladies, and it put large grins on our faces. It was always a relief when all clear sounded.

The next morning on our way to school, some kids found splinters from the bombs and shells, which were more exciting for the boys than us girls.

The population got tired getting up at night. School started two hours later if the air raids started after midnight. If the raids were before midnight, our school day started at the regular time, 8:00 AM. My aunt's apartment house had enough damage that they could not use the balcony anymore. The cracks in the walls and in the staircase were extensive but still safe enough to negotiate. The buildings are sturdier in Germany than they are here in the States. The windows in the cigar store on the first floor were broken from the air pressure the bombs created. Someone had pilfered cigars and cigarettes. The thief was shot in front of the store with the loot in his hands. Not many people tried stealing after that incident.

Every apartment house had a foreman who must see to it that the attics had boxes of sand and buckets with water to extinguish the smaller fires that were started by the firebombs. He had to stay in the house when the alarm sounded and I remember one soldier in the shelter sleeping while standing up. I had never seen anyone doing that before. Bunk beds were in the shelters for the elderly and the children to rest on or sleep. I remember the fear in Mom's eyes; it made me afraid too. When a bomb fell nearby, we ducked our heads between the shoulders. Some tried to make jokes; we laughed, but it was a nervous laugh. We were happy when the family was together at night and when we got a night's sleep without the alarm going off. If we had an alarm during school hours, we went to the basement where the coals were stored; those fumes made me feel nauseated every time we had to go in there.

My school was quite large. It was a two-story building, with the girls and boys separated. During recess, the school yard was divided too; there was no mixing of the sexes. Looking back, I believe it was the right thing to do. The children were not distracted as much and learned better. I wish we would implement it here. Some of the problems could be resolved and would not cost anything. All our schools had large gyms with ropes hanging from the ceiling, poles to climb, pommel horses, ladders, rings, and double bars. We learned how to use all of them. None in my class tried to climb the rope all the way to the top. My teacher warned me not to do it, but I did not listen. I just had to go up there. I had to touch the ceiling; it did not matter what the consequence might be if I disobeyed. It felt like I had accomplished something, and I believe she understood. I was not punished.

When I was ten years old, I had to join the Hitler Youth. I had time to enjoy activities away from home. We learned a lot of new songs, made toys for poor children, collected books and magazines to take to the hospitals where our wounded soldiers were recuperating. We entertained with song and dance at Christmas parties for our soldiers. We sold little wooden toy people that we could hang on our Christmas trees. Those were made in homes of the poorer mountainous regions, small businesses to improve the standard of living. I still have some of those. What I liked most of all was sports. I loved to run and was the fastest in my age-group. I could not throw a ball at any distance; it would always land sideways close to me.

Far jumping was my specialty; I could get to twelve feet and seven inches. Coaches from sport clubs were watching and invited me to participate at their facilities. When I joined, my highest jump was forty-two inches. When Mom learned that boys were in the club too, I was forbidden to go. Mom's fear made me miss a lot of things. Every year we had a sports fest and I always got a medal, a small one I could pin on my lapel. We had to wear a uniform to our meetings—a navy skirt and a white short-sleeved blouse and a black tie with a brown leather knot. Also, a brown jacket when weather was cooler. Mom did not have enough money to purchase a new one; I had to use an old one from a friend, with the color washed out in places. When a military parade was going through the town, we had to line the sidewalks and cheer our soldiers. Many times we would throw flowers in their path. I was happy participating; it was time away from babysitting my sister. I also learned how to use the fretsaw when we made toys for the poor children at Christmas.

When I was ten, Mom also took me to the theater with her. We dressed in our Sunday best. It was a big event for me to walk up the stairs to the theater with the large columns outside. Inside, there was red carpeting everywhere. The brass banister was shining like gold in the light of the chandeliers. The seats were also covered in red plush. It was the Christmas program, a wonderful performance of *Hansel and Gretel* from Humperdinck. I still see the scenes in my mind today. We could only afford standing tickets for the uppermost balcony. By the first intermission, Mom had discovered an empty seat for me and smuggled me there. She loved the theater; and later, when times were normal again, she would have season tickets for many years. She knew the music from every opera and operetta. The actor who played Santa Claus that night was Herman Messmer. His acting was superior. He frequented the restaurant across the theater, which my aunt and uncle now managed.

When we visited that establishment, we waited for Mr. Messmer to arrive after the performance. He loved to eat snails, and we watched with fascination and disgust as he swallowed them. At the time, the regular customers got only one linen napkin per week. It was kept in a special, fancy envelope with the guest's name on it. We were too bashful to ask Mr. Messmer for an autograph; I wish I had. My hometown theater was known as the jumping board to stardom. Many actors became famous after performing in my hometown.

A friend of mine had gotten a new dress. It was a shirt sleeve pattern with pockets and pleats opening below the pockets. Oh, how I yearned for a dress like that; this was more teenage-like. My birthday was not far away. As I awoke in the morning, Mom and Renate were still sleeping. I sneaked out of bed and tiptoed into the living room. I dared not turn on the light. My hands touched everything on the table. I was so disappointed when I felt fabric under my hands. All I could think of was that I had gotten something practical again. It made me so sad, and I went back to bed. Renate could not believe that I had no desire to go and check on my presents. When we finally went into the living room and turned on the light, my eyes shone. I smiled and silently begged for forgiveness. That fabric was a beautiful plaid, and Mom made that special dress for me later—the one I had admired so on my friend.

Around that time, my father came for a visit. We had not seen him after the divorce, which was about six years. Mom was at work, and I let him in our apartment. As always, Renate accepted him and the chocolate he brought right away. They had something in common. They liked to play games and always won. Smiling came easy for both of them. And both did not take life too seriously. I was more reserved; I did not touch the chocolate. I remembered the fighting and the commotion when Dad hit Mom so many years before. It had left a scar, a feeling of resentment I could not get over from one minute to the next. Renate had been too little to remember anything, and I had never talked to her about it, even when we wanted to put an ad in the paper looking for a dad. We had spent two whole days trying to put an ad together and, finally, gave up. We were afraid that Mom would not approve. My parents eventually did get back together again. My father's mother was very much in favor of it. We could see Dad only when he was on furlough. That gave me time to get slowly adjusted to the situation, to have a dad in my life again. He was on the eastern front all through the war. One time we did not hear from him for six weeks. His troop was encircled by Russian tanks before Moscow. They had to dig tunnels through the snow between the tanks to get out.

Mom got very sick that summer, and when there was no improvement after a week, she sent me to get a doctor. It was a Sunday, and I went to several doctors, but each had an excuse. Mom's dad saw me standing on a street corner, crying, and wanted to know what was wrong. He sent me home after I told him, and within an hour, a doctor was at our place. I had been to four doctors, and none had responded to my plea. Mom had pneumonia; she could not or would not go to the hospital because we would have been alone. Why did she not ask her father for help? Was she too proud?

Slowly she got better. When she was able to walk, her father told her to come to his slaughterhouse and bring a cup. He was a wholesale butcher who purchased the animals and slaughtered them and sold the meat to the different butchers in the city. They then made their own sausages from the meat. When Mom got there, he killed a calf and filled Mom's cup with the fresh blood. They added a little salt, and Mom drank it all. On her way home, she had to use all her willpower not to vomit. She knew if that happened, people on the street would call an ambulance and her children would be alone. She did keep it down, and she repeated the procedure for several weeks. At her next doctor's appointment, her doctor was surprised by how well she was doing. She told him what she had done; he said he could not have prescribed anything better. I think Mom was a genuine heroine.

Opa died of a stroke in 1941. All the good food he always ate, the freshly ground beef, the whisky for his second breakfast, the large amounts at mealtime—it had shortened his life. He was only sixty-one years old and must have weighed 260 pounds. He was over six feet tall and really did not look that large to me. He was very muscular, no flab.

All the nice presents we got from him for Christmas, it was all over. He had invited us children many times to Sunday dinner. Only us, his only grandchildren. Mom was never included. Why? I don't know. Did he not like my father? There were so many things I did not know. I know that he purchased all the furniture for my parents' apartment. He had also offered to purchase a barbershop for my father, but my father had declined the offer.

Looking back, I know my father did not want the responsibility of a business. He wanted to be taken care of and be able to follow his passion—playing cards with his friends. But I remember my grandfather counting his weekly earnings on Sunday mornings. Piles of silver coins stacked up and other piles were with paper money. I never saw that much money all at once. I also remember seeing him in his nightgown one night with a white nightcap on his head. He was bald and needed the extra warmth the nightcap could provide during the winter months. He looked taller to me that night and more like a character out of our children's books.

We did not have heated bedrooms then either. Ice would accumulate on the windows during the winter and stay on there for weeks. After I had started school, he wanted me to come to his house first and show him my report card. I would always get a five mark silver coin. When school had started, he had discouraged me; he said, "Don't go to school, they only spank you and it is boring." But he did have a twinkle in his eyes saying that.

He had given his stepdaughter a piano, and I loved to play the songs I knew. It was only with one finger, but it made me happy. I kept on hoping that we would get one too, but we never asked. He was such an imposing and intimidating figure. Most of all, we missed the large package of meat he would bring every weekend. Our meat ration stamps were cashed in on the end of each month. Now we were just like everyone else; we had to tighten our belts. Sometimes, when he had come back from his buying trips, he brought us a peacock feather. Or he would leave us children the sandwich he had not eaten that day. The sandwich did not taste as good as the one the rabbits got in our storybook. To them it was something special, and I always hoped that Opa's old sandwiches would taste extra good too, but they never did.

I had to lay down a wreath at his funeral. His fourth wife informed us three days after his death that he had died. That gave her enough time to arrange for minimum distribution of the inheritances to his children. It was enough to purchase a carpet for the living room and a sewing machine.

When the carpet was delivered, Mom rolled around the floor and laughed. She was so happy. We had never seen our mother acting so human, so uninhibitedly happy. And slowly, at first, we joined her on the floor; and then the three of us laughed and laughed till we got tired.

Mom was doing hand embroidery on knitted garments not too far away from our home. One sunny day, I decided to pick her up and keep her company walking home. I was a little late and noticed her on the other side of the street. She was wearing a blue summer dress and white linen shoes. My eyes followed her; she looked so young with her red hair bouncing up and down. I noticed for the first time that she was not only my mother but also a young woman. After I watched her for some time, I ran after her, holding on to her hand and talking to her made me happy.

My first-grade teacher died that same year of cancer. And I was elected to lay down a wreath at his funeral too. It was scary to see the casket being lowered into the floor. Every chapel at the graveyard had that arrangement. That's when it started; I had to lay down wreaths at funerals. I looked like the typical German girl with my blond braids and wearing that uniform. Not one person asked me if I might want to be removed from that job. No one should expect children to do that, but I did what I was asked to do.

Now Mom learned how to sew and how to use the sewing machine. A friend helped her along, and Mom was a fast learner. The sewing machine helped making our dresses a lot easier. Some nights she would sit up till morning to finish our outfits. When we opened our eyes in the morning, the dresses would be hanging on our wardrobe, ready to wear. When I was in fourth grade, she made me a nice skirt and vest with blue embroidery with a blouse, which I loved to wear. A little fabric was left over, enough for a hat, I thought. Mom made it and lined it with the blue remnants from another dress. She did beautiful work, but how to finish the front of the hat? I wish she had asked me, but we were told only to speak when asked, so I said nothing at first. At the time, children could be seen but not heard.

When she could not think of a way to do it, I spoke and told her how to make it work. I believe that confirmed her decision to let me learn to be a tailor. I wanted to be a teacher, a home economics teacher. My teachers told me that I had talent.

I also was good in math and was thinking of technical designing. But our generation's life took so many turns, I had to do a lot of other things before I could teach. And then only for thirteen years till I was seventy-two years old. That was the most satisfying job, besides being a mother. One of my students still sends a Christmas card to me every year. She appreciated what she had learned in my class.

Uncle Ernst, Mom's brother who was also a butcher, had been drafted when the war started. He was missing in action in Russia and was never found. He had been such a nice person, always kind and nice to his younger sister. Not like his father who had a loud voice and who shouted a lot. Uncle Ernst would take us for a ride in his wine-colored Mercedes sometimes. He was amused when Renate and I urged him to drive faster so a truck or another car could not pass us. I decided then that I wanted a car someday when I grew up.

We had not visited that often; but after I was many years in the United States, he visited me in my dream one night, just like Mom did after I moved to Arkansas. She stood at the foot of my bed. The lady that was with her said, "See, here is your daughter," and then they left. I was wide-awake. Mom's brother had just looked at me. In 1942, I took a private shorthand class. Most girls were older in my class, but I could learn just as fast. But I felt out of place; none of the girls talked to me. I was too young for them. I never needed shorthand later in my life.

The bombings increased; the alarm would sound day and night. It was 1943 now, and mothers with children were urged to live with relatives in the country. Others who had no families to go to were moved out of the city to smaller villages, closer to my hometown. Mom took half of our furniture with us; she reasoned that we would have at least something left if our apartment got bombed or vice versa. We moved to Ernstroda, where my father's parents lived and where we had spent our summer vacations every year traveling alone. At first, we stayed with Grandma and later moved in with her brother. He had a larger house where we could occupy two rooms. The change was quite easy for us. It was a relief to be able to sleep through the night and not be afraid during the day. A creek was flowing around the back of their house. It took us awhile to get used to the water rushing by. After the war, when their son Ernst came home, we had to move again. Then we missed the sound of the splashing water. By then it was something that had relaxed us and had put us to sleep.

We went to school in the village and had the same teacher my father and his sisters had so many years before. The school was very little with only four classrooms—two rooms upstairs and two on the bottom floor. Two older teachers taught all the children in the village. Each age-group had about four to ten students, and each teacher taught thirty children, four grades in one classroom. I enjoyed school. It was repetition for me; we had all the subjects in seventh grade. Here was my chance to make all As, especially since my uncle had promised me a violin if I made all As. We were graded differently in Germany those years, from 1 to 6. To get a 1, I had to have everything 100 percent correct. One wrong answer and our grade would be a 2. I never got the violin even with my perfect grade. Times were hard; I did not remind my uncle of his promise. I felt that I really had not earned it under the circumstances. We were six boys and girls in the eighth grade.

In Thuringia, people speak with a very heavy brogue, and a few of the boys would write the same way. Two of them asked me to grade their papers before they turned them in, which made me ask for a sandwich or a piece of fruit in return. I was hungry all the time, and I wonder so many times how Mom could cook so many good-tasting meals with the few groceries we could buy with our ration cards.

I also had to continue with my confirmation lessons, which were taught by our woman minister. She was in her late twenties and was loved and admired by us all. The village had a large house next to the church for her to live in. When she was the pastor, the church was filled to capacity every Sunday. Whether it was summer or winter, men, women, and children filled the church. The men would sit in the balcony, and the women and children sat on the benches on the bottom floor. Slightly dusty wreaths with the names of the fallen soldiers from World War I hung around the balcony. Our minister was a wonderful preacher.

Confirmation lessons started when a child was twelve years old. I had already attended classes in my hometown for seventeen months. It was the largest Lutheran church in our city, where I had been baptized also. In Ernstroda, I continued with my lessons and also joined the choir. Grandma's village had about 750 inhabitants and 250 evacuees from the larger cities.

Our church had been a wooden building in the eleven hundreds when she was first built. She burned down a hundred years later. After the fire, the church was rebuilt with fieldstones, complete with a real organ, a larger steeple, and three church bells. During the war, two of the bells had been confiscated by the government to be used for cannons. When the war was over, one of the bells was found in Hamburg, where all the bells had been shipped. It was called the bell cemetery. The bell was shipped back to the village; the second one was never found. Many times I would sing with the organist. She would sing alto and play soprano for me so I could stay in tune. We also had to sing at funerals, and sometimes nobody would show up, just Else and I.

Else was also the leader of the Hitler Youth in the village. They did not do as much as we did in the city. She was told that she could not lead the children if she kept on playing the organ. She did not have to think of what to do; she chose to play the organ in church.

The winter was great in Thuringia with lots of snow; everyone had skis. In the evenings, all the young unmarried people in the village would meet on the hills to ski or to use the sleds all tied together down the hills. The first time I went skiing, we just did cross-country for three hours. I loved it and was not ready to go home. I am glad that I did; the next morning I had so much chest pain that Mom called the doctor. He could not find anything wrong in my chest. After he asked me about my activities the day before, he knew. Three hours skiing for the first time had caused a bad muscle ache. During the summer evenings, the young people did the same; they met on top of the hills with musical instruments and sang. After sundown, we walked back home, our arms linked together, still singing till we reached our homes. The villagers, sitting outside or looking out the open windows, smiled at us. It was the same as they had done so many years before us too.

Our grandfather had worked in the doll factory during the winter months several years before we came. We found shoe soles for dolls in a trunk in the attic. Grandmother had two large blue-painted trunks in the attic, decorated with folk art flowers and the year they were made. Those hundred-year-old trunks were full of treasures for us. I made a lot of dresses for our relative's dolls and fabricated shoes. They told me so when I returned for my aunt's golden wedding anniversary so many years later. I had forgotten all about it. The second trunk was filled with all kinds of hats my grandmother had worn as a young girl and a young woman. Renate and I brought the hats down from the attic; it brought a smile to Grandma's face when she saw those treasured hats that made her think of times past. They were so attractive, nice, and flirtatious; I could picture her as a young girl, full of hope and expectations. And then life turns out different from what you had planned.

She looked always the same then. Dark dresses with two underskirts or underslips. The first one was white with a lace border on the valance. Then came the red one on top of the white one. That one was called an *Anstandsrock*, or a "modesty skirt," to hide the white one underneath. The outer skirt was a dark cotton print. She wore her auburn hair in a bun; she always wet the comb when she fixed her hair, and her scalp would shine through her hair. She looked always like a grandmother to us. But her eyes were different; she had amber eyes with little golden specks in them.

Beautiful eyes that none of us inherited. She had five children: one was born dead and the other son died when he was four years old. I never asked her what happened; I did not want to make her feel sad. In Germany, the plots in the graveyards can be purchased for ten years and then rebought for ten more years in the cities. In the country, you could buy it for twenty years the first time. When we were evacuated, the village cleared part of the cemetery for garden plots for us evacuees. Ours was right next to the graves of Grandma's children. Now we could plant vegetables to help with the meager ration cards. Mom made a great vegetable garden; everyone did. No one could find any weeds, only wholesome food.

After he was finished with the farmwork in the fall, Grandpa cut down trees in the forest. Mom would help him there too. We could not buy coal and had to do our cooking and heating with wood. Everybody could purchase just a certain amount of wood. The forest looked like she was swept with a broom. There were no branches lying around. No underbrush, no pinecones on the ground. The forest was picked clean by the village people.

I had to bring Grandpa and Mom something warm to eat for lunch. It was easy to find them in the winter when snow covered the ground. Opa had an injury from World War I. His lower leg was not reattached correctly. His right foot would come down at an angle, a track easy to follow in the snow. The food that I took to them was in a *kiepe*, a rectangular woven basket one wore on his back. Grandpa would put two pieces of a tree stem in there, and I collected branches to cover them up. That was always a heavy load to carry home. Sometimes I would get too tired and had to rest on the side of the road, my feet in a ditch. I could not take the *kiepe* off my shoulders because I would not be able to lift it up again. That I have back problems today comes as no surprise. At home I helped Mom a lot to chop the wood into smaller pieces to make it the right size for our little stove. Grandma had used the *kiepe* too when she took her homemade butter to market.

She had beautiful, decorated forms for the butter. That was before the war. During the war, they had to deliver all the milk to the dairy and use ration cards like everyone else.

So many of our young men died in the war, and their bodies came back, and the funeral had to be arranged. I had to recite a poem every time. There was never enough time to prepare for it. Summer or winter, the villagers would march to the cemetery. A band would be playing, and the mourners would sit in front of us. It was hard not to cry with them when I saw how heartbroken everyone was. One time my father was at the funeral; I could see him watching me out of the corner of my eye. He was hoping I would not forget the lines; I never did. So many poems I had to recite, and

I don't remember any. I guess the sadness of it all made me forget or made me want to forget. Too many people dead, too much sadness, too much sorrow to bear.

Maybe that was the reason I liked to cut up in class sometimes. I wanted to be liked by the classmates and not favored by the teachers. And in the fall, when it was time to slaughter our pig, I saved the pig's tail and brought it to school with a safety pin. As our teacher walked through the aisles, I followed him and pinned the tail on his coat. It had been my intention to take it off before going on recess. But like so many intentions that fail, this one did too. Outside the school yard, the children noticed and snickered. In desperation, I approached the teacher and took the tail off. I told him there was something on his coat and then flung the tail with the pin attached in a yard nearby. I was so ashamed when he said, "You are a good girl."

When I look back, I am surprised at how the memories flow back. The slaughter of the pig was awful. That pig seemed to know that it would get killed. It screamed so loud and so long, I had to cover my ears. One minute it was running around in the barnyard, and the next, it was hanging on two hooks and its insides were removed. We children watched from the living room windows. A bench, the length of the wall, was under the window, which made it convenient for us kids to look out. By lunchtime, the head was cooked, and we all sat down and munched on a slice of homemade bread and a slice of meat from the head, which had more fat than meat on it. We were so deprived of fat by then that our bodies needed it. When we had been still at home, I had separated the fat from the meat, kept it in the corner of my mouth, and then spit it into the toilet. My mother would have been upset had she known. This tasted wonderful to us then.

Confirmation was on March 6, 1944. Mom was able to get two different fabrics: a wine-colored one with little white flowers for the confirmation exam day and a navy dress for the confirmation the following week. The family came together for dinner. In the afternoon, the confirmed visited each others' families. At each one's parents, we had to taste the cakes the mothers had baked. There were cakes on large round sheets with all kinds of different fruits. All these cakes were prepared at home but had to be baked at the bakeries. To get them there, we had to balance one sheet on our head and hold the other one with one hand and push it into our waist to give it some hold. The sheets were about twenty-two inches in diameter. Each family had their own marker on the cake. Some just used a half eggshell; others had more elaborate markers.

Grandma used chestnuts for her cakes. The same when the bread was baked. Grandma would get up early in the morning to start making the dough. When I was around, I would take the loaves to the bakery. Grandma had round and oval woven baskets to put the bread dough in, which always left a nice pattern on the outside of the loaves. The trick was to get the loaves on the wooden paddle for the baker to push into the oven. In Old Salem in North Carolina, these paddles are called bread irons because they are made out of iron. In our village, the baker used a wooden paddle. I was lucky and able to do it right the first time. When the oven was first heated in the morning, a sheet with bread dough was baked first. It was just a thin layer with different fruits or bacon and onions on top. While those sheets baked, the oven reached the right temperature for baking the bread. We carried the sheets home, and everyone in the family gathered at my grandparents' to eat the cake—large still warm triangles, just like pizzas. Grandfather did not like to eat cheese or butter. If the plain coffee cake was all finished, he would take a slice of bread, pour some coffee over it and a teaspoon of sugar on top. When working in the fields, everybody got a slice of bread and a piece of sausage in their hand—plus tea, coffee, or water to drink.

In the evenings or on weekends, Opa played barber and cut men's hair. In the winter months, he would do it inside the house. During the summer, he did it outside in the backyard with the discarded tools my father had left him.

Grandma was able to get some duck eggs when a hen was breeding. She placed them under the hen, hoping she would breed them with her own chicks. From four eggs, only one duck made it. But the rooster and other hens would make the little duck's life miserable. They did not accept it. Grandma kept Ducky in the barn till the evening when all the chickens were in the coop. It would roam around the yard, but as soon as Grandma wanted to go inside, it followed her to the door and made a lot of noise; she had to find a solution. She took off her outer skirt and placed it on a footstool and little Ducky was happy. It had adopted my grandma as his mother. In the Christmas letter, Grandma mentioned that nobody wanted to eat the duck roast she had made, including her. They all felt sorry for little duck, and we did too. Everyone had gotten too attached to it.

CHRISTMAS IN GERMANY

It starts with the Advent season, the fourth Sunday before Christmas. Mom would buy an Advent wreath, wind a red ribbon around it, and insert four candles on the top. The wreath would hang from the ceiling in some houses, but ours would be in a special stand on the table, held up with four ribbons and a gold star on top of the stand. Every Sunday, one more candle was lit, and we had sweets in the afternoons, wrote letters to Santa, and thought about all the wishes we had.

On December 6, the children put one of their shoes in the window overnight in the hope that St. Nicholas would fill them up with some candy. It is such a nice custom that I did this with my children when they were little. Obviously they liked it so much that they did it with their children also. When my grandson was in kindergarten at the time, he asked his classmates what they found in their shoes. They had no idea what he was talking about and protested when they got home. They wanted to know why St. Nicholas did not bring anything to their house. The teacher heard complaints from the parents and had a lot of explaining to do about a custom she knew nothing about either. But Christmas is the most wonderful time of the year with all its customs.

Santa Claus comes on Christmas Eve in Germany. In our region, which is Lower Saxony, he is called *Weihnachtsmann*. I recall *Weihnachten* (Christmas) from 1933, when I was three years old. He came to our apartment, knocking on the door so loud that I got scared. I had to wear my blue apron that night; aprons were used during the day when we were playing, not to a special occasion like this, I thought, and I should find out later why. The lights flickered on the tree when Santa opened the door and burst into the room. This large man appeared with white hair and a red coat and a sack, and all that was in there were hazelnuts and walnuts, and he disappeared as fast as he came in. That's why I had to wear that apron, to hold the nuts. My apron was so full that many scattered all over the floor, and it took me awhile to gather them all up.

That year, Mom's dad gave me a doll carriage for a present. He was wearing a Santa suit too but forgot to change his shoes. I stared at the house slippers he was wearing and told him that he was grandfather, not Santa. They all thought that I was a pretty smart little girl. But I loved that doll carriage; it looked just like a real baby carriage. On the way home later that night, I stopped people on the street and showed them the new chocolate-brown carriage. Mom told me that I would push it in front of people if they didn't pay attention the first time. I can't believe I could have been that aggressive.

After my sister was born, we followed the same ritual every year. Christmas Eve we had to spend all day in the kitchen while Mom was busy in the living room. The door was locked and the window in the door was covered with a cloth. I tried to stand on my toes, which did not help; I could not see anything. The same with the keyhole; that was covered too. We just listened and could hear Mom walk back and forth. She decorated the tree with icicles and all the multicolored glass balls we used every year.

Chocolate rings with different fillings and wrapped in pretty foil were also put on the tree. Those chocolate rings we would pick off the tree during the first week, but we always missed some. We found them later when we took the decorations off the tree. It was exciting to discover them later; it sweetened the good-bye from the Christmas season. Did Mom plan it that way? We also used real white wax candles. My rich friends had electric candles on their trees, but I liked to smell the aroma and watch the flickering of wax candles. Mom always told us not to go near the tree when she left the room while the candles were burning, and we obeyed. We kept busy in the kitchen blowing holes in the ice-covered windows while Mom worked in the living room. December is a very cold month of the year, and most times, snow is covering the ground. It was hard to concentrate on any game for long; the expectations were too high. Many groans escaped our throats while we were waiting.

Most stores closed at lunchtime on the twenty-fourth. The bookstore in our neighborhood stayed open till 6:00 PM. Mom would send me there every year to get a newspaper. As much as I hurried every year, I would always miss Santa. When I came home with the paper, Mom would say, "Santa was here while you were gone." Then she rang a little handbell; the door opened to the living room, and we could admire the tree in all its splendor.

The church bells started ringing all over the city at 6:00 PM also. Mom had three jobs after her divorce, so we stopped going to the Christmas service. She did not have enough time to do everything. Every church had real bells, some only four, but most of them six to twelve and more. The churches were calling to come to the service, calling in the Christmas night. It was such a holy sound that we just became still and listened and remembered the baby Jesus. I miss the ringing of the bells so much; Christmas is the time I miss my homeland the most. As much as I like it over here, and as much as I tried to make the holidays nice for my family, I always feel sad and get homesick. I've been living here for fifty-eight years, and I still get emotional about the Christmas holidays.

Our presents were not wrapped in paper; they were laying under the tree. After all the presents were inspected and Mom was hugged, we sat down for the traditional Christmas dinner, which consisted of goose with red cabbage, mashed potatoes, and a salad. Later, we would peel an orange. Mom could peel the orange so it looked like a rose. We always watched her hands as she performed that task. Chocolate, marzipan, and nuts tasted good with the orange. After washing our hands, we snuggled into Mom's arms, and she would read from the new book we had gotten from Santa. There were so many books over the years. When I could read a book, I would forget the whole world around me. It would cause problems at times when I was supposed to watch my sister and she had run off somewhere without my noticing.

Mom was a good reader and storyteller. She would tell us about her youth, when she had to read to her classmates during World War I. The children had to knit socks for the soldiers in their needlework classes. Our mother was also a very good and fast knitter, but as a child, her teacher made her read to the class while the other children were doing the knitting. She could make every story sound so real. Or she would sing for the class; she had a beautiful voice. Her favorite song was "Die Bluemelein sie schlafen im Mondschein" (The flowers are sleeping in the moonshine). It was played at her funeral in 2007, and everyone who knew her loved it. On Christmas Day, the children in our house would bring out the toys, and we would admire everyone's presents. We have two holidays at Christmas and Easter; also, Pentecost is celebrated for two days in Germany.

When I started first grade, half the children in the class believed in Santa Claus. The ones that had older siblings did not. Our teacher explained everything nicely to us. We had to promise not to tell our smaller siblings at home, which made us feel so much older that we knew and our sisters or brothers still believed.

My mom's dad always made large presents, like the dollhouse, which I liked to decorate and where my sister would always rearrange everything as soon as I was leaving the room. It even had a toilet in the bedroom that we could flush. After the newness had gone, I lost interest. The store he gave us was something Renate and I could both play with at the same time. All the drawers contained candy that looked like lentils, beans, or noodles. There were cereal boxes on the shelves, marzipan sausages on the counter, and ham and eggs made from marzipan. We also played with a real scale and a register that worked. That was fun for many years. Grandfather had a large tree in his dining room that reached all the way to the ceiling. That room was not heated during the week; that's why his tree would last so much longer than ours. French doors led from the living room into the dining room, and they would open slowly like magic. Renate could not get in fast enough. He had electric lights on his tree, and the tree would turn slowly and play "Silent Night." Mom said they had that tree stand already when she was still at home. I remember the presents and the food, but I don't remember any hugs and kisses. He must have loved us, but he just could not show it like so many people during those years. When I was a baby, he lifted me up proudly in his hand and was delighted when I had wet my diapers and, since they were cloth diapers then, also his hand.

Mom never talked about the holidays from her childhood; why, Mom? Probably having had three stepmothers made the difference. Mom's mother had died when Mom was four years old. Her father married again and divorced that woman. The next wife died, and with the fourth wife, he died. So Mom and her sisters had to go to work, taking care of other families as soon as they had finished school. Mom's older sister, Tony, died when she was twenty-two years old. I never met her. But I met Mom's grandmother. She had pretty curly white hair. I recall seeing her in a black dress that came all the way to the floor. She would sit me on her lap and move her legs from one side to the other and sing dideldum. I called her Dideldum Oma. She was also the one that wrote a play when she was eighty-nine years old. And I remember Mom telling me that the play was performed, but I don't know where.

When we were evacuated in 1943, Christmas was a little different, but I liked it just as much. My paternal grandfather would take care of the trees in the woods during the winter months. The village was surrounded by woods. He would select only perfect trees that would fit in the houses in his village and only as many as were needed. Every family had about the same-sized tree, or they put in a special order for a slightly larger one.

Grandpa knew where to find the best trees. He had planted most of them in the "tree schools," which is what he called them, a fenced-in area where the new seedlings were first planted. Two weeks before Christmas, he got someone to help him. Both men cut the trees and then brought them into the village on a big sled. The sled was pulled up the mountain by a cow. On the way down, the men steered the sled by hand. They had to hold on to the brakes with all their might so that the sled would not get out of control. As soon as they were in the valley, the cow began pulling the load again. The trees were placed around Grandpa's house, and I was permitted to sell them. I had lots of fun doing it, and Grandpa let me keep the tips. At the time, there was not much to buy anymore; the presents were mostly homemade. That grandpa did not give hugs and kisses either. After the holidays, he would cut off the top of the tree to where the branches came out; he peeled off the bark and cut the branches off at about an inch from the stem. After that, he cut the main stem off about ten inches and smoothed the wood; this made a stirring spoon for Grandma. It is called a *quirl* in Germany (see picture). We used them when making pudding or when we thickened gravies. I wish I had one of those today.

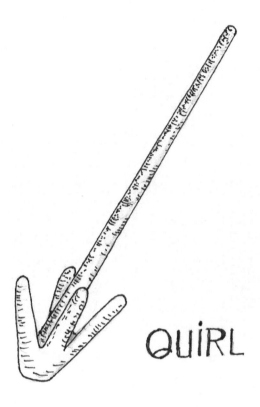

QUIRL

I have only one of his carved wooden pipes, with a deer head, which he used on Sundays. He had several pipes hanging under a "What Not" in his living room. The longer pipes with painted porcelain heads he used for leisure times and the shorter ones for smoking during the day. By the end of the war, the farmers all grew some tobacco for their own use. He cured his in the niches of his large red tile oven in the living room. That oven was heated from the kitchen. Grandma could cook in it in the kitchen and heat the living room at the same time. I loved to sit with my back against the oven in the winter, and so did my cat.

On Christmas Eve, the whole family went to church when the bells started ringing. A large oven stood in the sanctuary. A wooden fire was lit in the oven early in the morning to warm the church some. We still needed to wear our coats; it usually would get extremely cold there. All the eighth graders would be singing in the choir. Sometimes the older boys would help ring the bells, and others had to pump the organ. We had a real organ with shiny pipes in the back of the church. After the church service, we would go home, and the whole family had dinner together. Goose or duck, red cabbage, and instead of mashed potatoes, we had potato dumplings, a specialty in that region. The dumplings were made from raw potatoes, which always took a lot of time to make. We had to peel a twelve-liter pail of potatoes and then grate them, everything by hand. We did not have all the electric appliances then as we have now. After that the liquid had to be pressed out of the grated potatoes, which was done with a press. The dry raw potatoes were mixed with some cooked mashed ones; some salt was added, and they were formed into dumplings as large as your fist. Before inserting them into lightly boiling water, some croutons were put into the middle of each dumpling. They would start floating to the top when done. I'm getting hungry for some as I write this down. Grating the potatoes always took some skin off our fingers; that always hurt. The squeezed-out water from the potatoes had to stand for several hours before we could pour it off. What was left was potato flour, which we used just like cornstarch today, for thickening our gravy.

I don't remember what kind of presents we received. Times were hard, and we were just happy to be alive. I know I made house slippers for family and friends across the street from the plush fabric from the railroad cars.

Pincushions I had made too from leftover fabrics. When I went back after thirty-six years for my aunt's golden wedding anniversary, my friends and relatives showed me the pincushions I had made for them so many years ago. I had always kept busy in my spare time with sewing, knitting, or crocheting. They had saved all these items for so many years, which touched me deeply. They kept doll clothes I had made for our friend's children too, inspired by the hundred-year-old chest in the attic where we discovered shoe soles, left over from the time when grandfather had worked in the doll factory. The farmers would take different jobs during the winter months when there was no fieldwork to do. I have seen a doll at the antique road show that was made in a village about three miles away from our village. That doll was worth eight hundred dollars. Our dolls were given to us from our father's parents. We had many beautiful dolls, my Mom always gave them new dresses for Christmas every year. We sold the dolls in 1947 to British soldiers to finance our move back to West Germany. After we started school, we had to learn a new poem about Christmas every year and had to recite it in front of the tree before we could look at the presents.

Stores were not open on Sundays and on Saturdays at lunchtime. Around 1950, the stores were open again for two Sundays. The two weeks before were called Silver Sunday, and the following week, it was called the Golden Sunday. Everyone in the store had to work in the sales department. By then the stores were filled with everything again, like before the war. It was expensive, but people started buying again. We had the best time on those days. Everyone was in a good mood. Since it was always so cold, the adults would drink a *Gluehwein* (a hot punch) to keep warm. A glass of hot red wine mixed with some water, a piece of cinnamon, a slice of lemon, and some sugar—that definitely contributed to the jolly mood in the population. At lunchtime, we all were served a nice dinner, and at year's end, everyone would receive a whole month's wages extra—a Christmas bonus.

Several Christmases stand out in my mind, and they're not the ones when I was little. When I was working in the large department store in our city, the stores closed officially at lunchtime, but the alteration department had to stay open longer many times because there was always a customer who needed something done at the last minute. Sometimes it would take till 5:00 PM before we could leave and go home. And when we chatted a little before saying good-bye, it was time to follow the ringing of the church bells. I went to the service, and as I was leaving the church, snow had fallen, and it kept on snowing as I walked home. Hardly anyone was on the street, just a few stragglers. The lights were coming in on the windows; one after the other you could see people light the Christmas trees; the holy night had started. It was so peaceful. There were no cars on the street, and the trolley cars were running only once every hour. The snow stayed on the ground and sparkled like millions of tiny diamonds in the light of the street lanterns. Each step would make a crunching sound, a sign that the snow would stay for a while and that we would have a white Christmas. It reminded me of a poem we had learned about the holy night.

Those are the things I see in my mind when I think of Christmas in Germany today—the peace and quiet and the snow on the streets glistening. And of course, the Christmas market, which starts four weeks before. We did not have it during the years we were evacuated, but it slowly started after the war to its present splendor. It is a wonderful tradition—the smell of the lebkuchen (spiced cakes), waffles, bratwurst, all the many crafts, Christmas decorations, and the hot punch we would drink to keep us warm. As children, we would go window-shopping downtown and spread out our arms in front of the store windows and declare it all belonged to us. The stores had wonderful animated decorations from all of the children's stories on display.

As I was getting older, I had to do extra chores to make some money for Mom's present. She would check later if there was any dust left around the feet of the stove in the kitchen. Mostly I did forget cleaning there. Mom always said to me, "You think, if you place a clean tablecloth on the table, the kitchen is clean." She was so right. I loved hand-embroidered linens and still do today. And it was always the first thing I did, putting a freshly starched tablecloth on the table. I have made so many over my lifetime and won prizes at the state fairs here in the States for my handcrafted items. Mom's friend would go shopping with me to choose a present for Mom. She would steer me in the right direction, where we could find something practical for her. When I was younger, I would probably have purchased something frivolous for my mother. Seeing Mom's pleasure in her eyes was all worth it.

And then the New Year arrived with its special foods, herring salad, hard rolls, and punch bowl. Pouring hot lead into water to see what kind of forms would emerge that would tell of the future. When the church bells rang at midnight, trumpeters would blow their trumpets on top of city hall, and almost everyone would have fireworks to celebrate the New Year. The noise reverberated between the houses and would last over an hour before all was quiet again. A dog followed my father home on one New Year's Day, a black schnauzer. He was so cute, just like the one we had in one of our storybooks. We were so happy and were hoping nobody would inquire about him. Mom did check the paper every day, and sure enough, someone was looking for our dog. As Mom walked him to his house a week later, he started pulling on his leash, eager to get to his old home. She could tell he had lived there before. The owner was happy to get him back. She told Mom that he had run after a firecracker exploded on New Year's Eve, which had scared him. It also had impaired his hearing. This happened in 1948. It was sad for us to lose him, but we also were grateful that we had him for one whole week. That experience later made me get a dog for my children when they were still young. He was half poodle and half

Manchester terrier. Roger was about six or seven years old at the time; and Tom, three years older, had fun with Pooch, as we called him. Roger would ask us many times why Poochy's mother jumped over the fence and why he was half poodle and half Manchester terrier. He did not understand what the saying meant. It amused us over many years. Poochy had to be put to sleep when he was sixteen years old. He needed a third kidney operation, which he would not have survived according to the vet. The years with him had been a lot of fun; he had enriched our lives.

MY YEAR OF DUTY FOR THE FATHERLAND

After graduation from public school, the children that could not afford higher education had to work one year for a family with at least four children or for a farmer. This helped with the war effort since all the younger men had been drafted. I was sent to work for a farmer in the next town, only three miles away from our village. He was a *Fuhrunternehmer*, a carrier with a horse-drawn wagon who would bring in the harvest for some people. He also drove people around in a carriage: a horse-drawn carriage in the summer and a sleigh in the winter. I had no idea what was involved; I just thought, *At least I get enough to eat.* I should have found out differently. I had just turned fourteen, was still growing, and had a healthy appetite. The contract stated that I should get two weeks' vacation, attend school one day a week, have every second Sunday off and a free day every two weeks.

The start was not too bad; my boss would forget my name in the morning. He would call up the stairs before he went to the stable. That meant another half hour sleep for me since he didn't want to call out the wrong name. The day started in the morning at five, and after ten at night, I had time for myself, which meant going to bed since I was too tired to do anything else. My room was on the third floor, a small dormer with a window toward the barn. It was a sparsely furnished room without a table lamp; I could not read anything in the evening—the one thing I really enjoyed. But then I was too tired from the day's work anyway.

My duties were to milk the cow by hand twice a day and feed the cow, calf, swines, chickens, rabbits, and ducks. I also cleaned the house, which meant washing and waxing the floors. If I did not bend forward enough when polishing the floors, the lady of the house would hit me on the back. I was polite to her; but in reality, I feel she was not a lady and did not deserve the title. She only did the cooking and grocery shopping. She was very good at repairing her husband's long johns. She patched them up with fabric from an older pair. They looked like riding pants after she finished. I wanted to compliment her and told her she was doing a wonderful job. She said, "I teach you if you stay another year with us." That happened later in the winter, and my reply then was, "No, thank you." Every time my boss had to take customers for a ride, either with the sleigh in winter or the carriage in the summer, I had to polish the brass decorations on the harness. The hoofs of the horses had to get a coat of black grease. I was scared every time I had to crawl under the horses to do this. They looked mighty big when I sat under their bellies; I was scared to get trampled on, and I still feel the apprehension I had then. I was a girl from a large city who had never done this before and had never seen anyone else do it either. I had never been that close to a horse before. A brass hot-water bottle also needed polishing in the winter. It was used on the sleigh with a large black-bear blanket to keep the customers warm.

The large vegetable garden had to be tilled. We had no tiller, so I had to dig with a spade, which took several days. Later the fruit needed harvesting, which was a sweet labor. Many of the berries made it into my mouth. I loved the goose berries, black berries, and currants, the red ones more than the black ones. We had strawberries and all kinds of vegetables. Hay was made twice during the summer. In between, we cut some fresh grass for the animals. Collecting potato peels and leftover food from several hotels was my job too. Those leftovers had to be prepared for the pigs to eat. Cleaning the pigsty was another job I hated to do. I tried to hold my breath when I was in there, but the stench was always pretty bad.

The war had lasted already so long that we did not have many clothes to wear, especially when one was a growing child. The few things I had were pretty. I was not allowed to wear my own clothes; I had to wear Mrs. Bellman's skirt, old apron, and blouse from the early twenties. The first thing I did was shorten that skirt by about seven inches, but I was immediately told to let the hem out again. When I complained to my mother about it, she said, "Just put up with it, that year will pass too. I don't want the villagers to think we are complainers." But that was not all; the shoes I had to wear were cutoff rubber boots, too large for me. Oh! I was so ashamed to run around like that. I know where my love for shoes comes from today. It all goes back to the time when I had to do without or when I had to wear those cutoff rubber boots.

The one nice day during the week was Friday, school day. We had a good teacher, and I looked forward to those days. We learned how to cook and clean, how to be good housewives, how to run a business, how to write checks, and how to keep up with math. You would call it home economics here. It also gave me time to make friends in class, to talk to someone my own age.

One day, about lunchtime, the alarm sounded, something I thought we had escaped from. Before we could get to the ground floor and decide whether or not the situation was serious, the bombs started falling. I had never seen this before. Just like the movies, one after the other fell down—a little slanted, bringing destruction. We went downstairs really fast, and everyone who lived in the back houses and the lady from the store downstairs tried to open the large door to the street. The planes were flying low over the house and shooting at the older men in the backyard who wanted to get a better look. Several were wounded that day. I closed the door as fast as I could, and as soon as the plane disappeared over the house, I opened the door. We all went across the street into the air-raid shelter unscathed.

We could see burning houses when all clear sounded, and Mrs. Bellman told me to go to her daughter's house to see if she was all right. Her daughter lived on the other side of town in a beautiful villa. It would take me about fifteen minutes to walk there. But first, I encountered a bucket brigade. A house, which had been hit by a bomb, was burning; and the street was piled high with rubble. Climbing over it, I had to walk through a line of people, and for a while, I passed on the buckets but then broke the line and went farther. It made me feel guilty not helping them, but I did have to leave.

It was so sad to see the beautiful villa in ruins. The sidewalls had just collapsed under the pressure of the bombs, and the roof was resting on all the rubble. Two ladies died in the basement; their lungs burst from the air pressure the bombs created when they hit the house. It looked like they were sleeping, sitting in lawn chairs. The lady on the third floor, who was resting on her sofa and nursing a broken leg, flew with her sofa over two rows of large trees across the street and into the front yard of those houses. She landed safely, still resting on her couch. She was just shocked over the sudden transport. But the daughter and granddaughter of Mrs. Bellman, that beautiful five-year-old girl and the daughter who was so nice and kind to everyone, not at all like her mother, had died on the way to the basement. That day and the next, we were all trying to dig them out, and our mind played tricks on us. We believed we could hear their voices crying for help. It is something you want to hear; you cannot bear the thought of them lying under the rubble dead. You hope against all hope and keep on digging. The third day we found pieces of the braids, a hand, and other body parts; and the Bellmans sent me home. They thought I should not see any more of this, and I was grateful. Knowing they were buried under the rubble and finding pieces of them when digging through the rubble was a horrible thing. I hope and pray that I never have to witness anything like that again in my life.

Forty people were killed in that air raid; and several weeks later, they were buried in four mass graves, ten caskets in each. I had to lay down a wreath of flowers on the caskets. The four graves were divided by about twenty inches of earth, four rectangular holes in the ground. How could they dig them so perfectly? If I had gone alone toward the casket, maybe it would have been okay; but other people followed me, and the earth collapsed while four of us slid down to the caskets. I was the last one to be brought up, and the people said, "Those will be the next ones that will be killed." My mom arrived just as it happened and was just as upset as I was. That day I cried all day, I could not stop; the tears flowed and flowed.

One plane had been shot down in that air raid. The pilot landed with his parachute in the trees across the street. The people tried to get him out of the tree. If the police had not come in time to free him, I believe that he would have been lynched; people were that angry. On a walk through the woods during my lunch break at school the week after, I found a glove. It was a glove from a fighter pilot; it looked like a new glove. I was scared to pick it up. I figured there must have been at least two people in the plane. Had the other one been wounded? Was this his glove? Was his hand still in the glove? Where was the other pilot? Was he hiding in the woods? Where was his plane? I did not touch the glove, and the following week when I looked for it again, the glove was gone.

The closet in my room was now full of Mrs. Bellman's daughter's beautiful clothes, which we had dug out of the rubble. There were shoes, at least fifteen pairs, of all styles and colors. I tried some of them on; they fitted perfectly. The shoes were purchased in the most expensive stores. Sometimes I thought Mrs. Bellman did this on purpose to torture me. I just looked; I did not take anything and did not ask for anything. I was too proud. Her son-in-law had walked with me on the street one day when he was on furlough. He, in his impressive uniform, and I, in the old hand-me-downs and cut-off rubber shoes, was pulling a handcart to collect potato peels from the hotel. He told me that he did not like his mother-in-law either. This, along with the bar of chocolate he gave me, impressed me very much. When I visited Austria in 1986, our tour took us to Salzburg for a nice program about the Wiener waltz. When I heard the announcer, I knew it was he, the son-in-law of my former boss. I talked to him at intermission time, and he told me I had the wrong person, but he never looked me in the eyes while I talked to him. I let him know that I appreciated his kindness so many years ago and left, feeling sure it was he. My guess was that he lived under another name; or is my imagination running away with me?

Another time my boss poked me with a pitchfork while unloading freshly made hay. I was in the upper loft of the barn. The opening was very small, and I could not see where the fork came up and he could not see where I was standing. I waited for a while, but when the bleeding did not stop, I went to the doctor. He had been retired and started working again after his daughter was drafted. The wound had all the dust and seeds from the hay in it; it did not look good. He prescribed a pink ointment, the same as my grandmother used for her rheumatism. I used it that night, and about two in the morning, I heard our neighbor calling my name and asking what was wrong. I had been crying while sleeping.

It was a warm summer night, and the windows were open. I had cried in my sleep about the pain in my leg. The neighbor told me to go downstairs and show the Bellmans my leg, which I could not do: I was locked in. The key was missing on my door. I went back to sleep, and when I awoke at five in the morning, the key was back in my door and the door was not locked. What had happened? I knew it was not a dream. Descending the stairs, I overheard Mrs. Bellman talking to her son, asking, "Do you want to do this

again?" When I walked into the kitchen, they stopped talking, which gave
me an uneasy feeling. I told my mother and aunt about it on my next visit.
My aunt told us that the son had raped a girl two years before. I had always
liked my father's sister, but after that incident, I never took the affection she
displayed toward me as real. This was not a situation you allowed anyone
to get into, least of all one's own niece and godchild. How could she? That's
why Mrs. Bellman made me wear those old-fashioned clothes. She wanted
me to look unattractive for her son. Mrs. Bellman's son got married a few
months later, and from all the cakes that were baked for that wedding,
I got two pieces. Mrs. Bellman preferred to hoard food and let it perish
rather than be generous to others. These were the people who employed
me for a whole year for twenty marks a month, which I put in my savings
account. I could not withdraw any money for years after the Russians came
and occupied that part of Germany. The money was devaluated years later,
and we could withdraw small amounts after that. I felt like a slave working
there. After three days, just when I thought I could not take the pain in my
leg any longer, I could see a pink ring around the wound. It was healing;
and the ointment had cured the infected flesh without antibiotics, which
had not been developed then, but with a lot of pain.

One hot summer day while making hay, a soldier came by and started
talking to me. His parents had a farm, and he wanted to help. He was
recovering from a war injury, and since he was feeling better, he yearned
for some work. I told Mrs. Bellman, and the next day I brought an extra
sandwich and a rake, and he was there again to help me. There were no
people in the fields and nobody walked by; I wish I knew how my mother
found out that a soldier was helping me. The same happened when I had
my braids cut off. She came to town the next day and scolded me. I had
asked to have them cut off for months; and the last time, she had not said
no, which I took for a yes—my first defying act that upset her. When
you are fourteen in Germany, you are a fräulein. It's something you look

forward to. Before, we girls had to curtsy when saying hello to an adult. Now we too were curtsied by the younger children. It was not so easy to get used to. I thought if I was fourteen and a fräulein (miss), I also should not have to wear braids anymore. The short hair did not look good on me; I was not used to putting my hair into curlers and had no time to do so. What I needed was a perm, and only sixteen-year-olds or older could get them then. But I was lucky; a girl in our village had to cancel her appointment, and I could use hers. I really felt good with my look after and always looked sideways in the store windows whenever I passed one to admire myself. Looking back, it must have been Mrs. Bellman who called my mom and told her about my haircut and the soldier.

One week before that year came to an end, I packed my few possessions and just left, without saying good-bye. I lost my pay for that month because of it, but it was worth it for me. That week was my vacation. I ran all the way home, barefoot to save my shoes. The meadow next to the railroad tracks were soft, carpeted with thick grass, which cushioned my feet. Arriving home, I was so hungry that I ate half of the cake Mom had baked with potatoes. It was a mushy cake but tasted okay. Renate said, "Sigrid is eating all our cake." She had no idea how hard I had to work and how little food I had been given. She was a puny eater and always looked two years younger than her actual age. But I did feel guilty after that. About two years later, I met Mrs. Bellman on the street, and she asked me to please come back. She said, "No one stays with us anymore." I told her I was not surprised and said, "No, thank you."

THE AMERICANS ARE COMING

The war would be ending soon. The Americans landed in Normandy. People were breathing a sigh of relief. You couldn't talk about it. You might whisper to your friends. The concentration camps were scary places to go too. You never knew if somebody would report you to the officials. Some of the German soldiers were coming back from the eastern front. All wanted to be captured by the Americans. People gave them civilian clothes if they had something that would fit them. They stayed one or two nights, and they walked away, traveling mostly by night.

Our village was attacked by air several times more. After the war, we learned that there was a cave between our village and the next city where the military worked on some kind of secret. The British knew about it, but the bombs never fell too close to that cave. No one ever noticed any military forces in the woods. Usually, our Sunday walks would not take us that far anyway. During the week, no one noticed any extra traffic or transports to become suspicious about.

But the British attacked, dropped bombs, shot at the people in the streets. It did not matter if you were an adult or a child. A relative and her child were shot as she was standing at the window, a dumb thing to do, but this was all new to them. We had experienced already so much worse in my hometown. In one air raid, I had to pass about ten houses to get into the air-raid shelter, which was in our doll factory. The plane came down and tried to shoot me while I was pressing myself into the entrances of each house so they would not see me. He would circle and come back three times. I did make it to the shelter unharmed, and Mom was glad to see me, but her eyes were showing much fear. When you are young, the thought of dying, or how and when it could happen, does not enter your mind. But you are scared and speak a silent prayer. Most bombs fell into the fields; we would go there later to see how much of an impact they had made.

I decided to work for a farmer in our village; they needed someone and were real nice people. The Dartmans were so nice I would have worked for free. The food was not locked away; I could eat when I was hungry. Just the opposite, the Dartmans thought I was too skinny and always wanted me to eat more. They had a larger farm and more animals. I had to milk three cows twice daily. Those twelve-liter buckets could get quite heavy when they filled up with milk. Paul Dartman would always proudly tell everyone that I milked three cows and that I was a city girl. What a difference it makes when you get a compliment once in a while. They had four pigs, two goats, sixty rabbits, three cows, one calf, and that big ox, the largest in the village. Paul was very proud of his ox. He could hardly reach the top of his back when brushing him. And of course, there were lots of chickens and a mean rooster. Mrs. Dartman helped me getting the eggs out of the henhouse by dropping a basket over the rooster's head. She had to hold it down while I went into the henhouse to collect the eggs. She had many bruises on her legs from the rooster's former attacks. You can get bruises just from being hit by the rooster's wings. The cows would not always behave either. That tail would swish back and forth when the flies were too plentiful. When you milk by hand and sit there with your head leaning against the cow's belly, you can get hit in the face by the tail. It hurts when the long tail hair flings itself around your head. I made sure that the tails were washed often.

Paul liked to tease me too, like chasing me around the farm with his bullwhip, cracking it to my right and my left, and he just laughed when I begged him to stop. When you know that cracking the whip can exceed the speed of sound, my fear to get hurt was well-founded. He also let go of the goat one day while he cleaned its sty. I had been teasing her, pulling on her horns while she was tied to a chain. As soon as Paul loosened the chain, that goat started chasing me around the manure pile, which was very funny for him but not for me. Luckily, I was a fast runner and could barely escape into the house. A collision with those horns would have inflicted a lot of pain. The noise when she hit the door told me so. But he was delighted when I did something to him too, like pushing him unexpectedly when he was standing deep in thought.

As the noise of shooting guns came closer, the older men in the village went out one night and combed the woods for soldiers or some boys who might want to defend the village. They found none, and we were all relieved, though it scared me to be alone in the house that night. We wanted the Americans to occupy us. Every evening during the week, our village crier would stop on every street corner and ring his handbell. The people either looked out of their windows or front doors, waiting for his announcements. He informed them of special news concerning the village and its people. He also let folks know if the fertilizer had arrived and had to be distributed. News from the war or that some fees were due. That they had found some potato beetles, and the people had to go and check their fields. Of meetings that took place in the village. That evening, it was what everybody had expected for some time. The Americans were close, and the grocery stores were distributing all the dry goods the next morning. After getting the messages, the people would talk awhile and then return to their chores. Many years before, the crier was the village policeman, a helper for the mayor. I went early to the grocery store the next day, but lots of people were already in front of me. Our village had two stores, one in the lower village and the other in the upper village. The five steps leading up were also full of people. I was all the way in the back when all of a sudden, we could hear the rumbling sound from jeeps and tanks rolling into our village from a side street. I hollered "The Americans are coming," and in no time the store emptied, and I was the only customer left. Before I was served, everyone had come back to get their groceries first. The tanks and jeeps had stopped in front of the mayor's office, and the children surrounded the soldiers and were happy to get chewing gum. Two fräuleins were standing close too.

My boss told me to go home to my mother; she had fainted in the other store when she saw the Americans driving through the village. It's amazing how fast news gets around in a village when no one has a telephone. At the time, only business people had the luxury of a phone. It is funny to me today as I write this, but during that time, I was scared. We all were scared, did not know what to expect next. The daughter of a neighbor volunteered to go with me in the upper village were my mother lived. As we walked slowly and cautiously toward the mayor's house, two GIs jumped into a jeep and drove toward us. That was all I needed to turn around and run as fast as I could back to the Dartmans. The other girl could not keep up with me. Paul said later he never saw anyone run that fast before. I thought that was my best time ever too, and none of the soldiers had followed us. If those guys had driven on the street instead of on the sidewalk, I probably would not have reacted that way; but driving toward us on the sidewalk could only spell trouble for me—or so I thought. Later that evening before it got dark, I tried again to see Mom, but went the back way, behind the village, hoping the soldiers would not know that there was a grassy path. I got to her house safely. Mom was all upset; people said she was the first one who hung out the white sheet, which she denied. Every house had the sheets hanging out the windows, which meant we were giving up. An act like that meant treason and was punished with death. Renate was scared that Mom would find the hatchet she had hidden. Mom had said sometime before that she would kill her if the soldiers started raping people. Rumors abounded; everyone was afraid of rape, which did happen quite often.

The mayor embarrassed himself too. He said "Heil Hitler" when he faced the American commander. "We are not defending the village." It seems so funny now. He was teased about that remark for many years. The GIs would come into our houses and ask for Nazi paraphernalia. If we said we did not have any, they would come in and look in our closets and open our drawers to check if we told the truth. Most people had destroyed things like that a long time ago. Now you could get rid of those things; the war was almost over. Sometimes the GIs would give coffee or cigarettes for souvenirs. Really good things like silverware were often buried in the backyards or under the potato bins in the basements. The first group of soldiers occupied the lower village. The farmers were allowed to be in their houses to take care of the animals and do some farmwork later on during the day. At night, after the 8:00 PM curfew, they had to stay with families in the upper village. I never met the soldiers that stayed at Grandma's house. She said that they were real nice.

One evening, two soldiers knocked on our door, asking if we could cook coffee at 10:00 PM after they were finished patrolling the streets. They would bring the coffee, and we should supply the cake. The farmers had always enough eggs and butter to bake cakes; it was us city people that had to live strictly on ration cards that made us go hungry all the time. At least it would keep us slim, no excess weight. Fifteen minutes after ten we heard the knock on the door, and we young ones scurried upstairs while the older generation went into the kitchen and cooked coffee. What a smell, the aroma of real coffee wafting up the stairs. Not like the coffee we had to drink all these years that was made from roasted grain. Even I could tell the difference. We girls were sitting upstairs, looking through the banister, and trying to catch some of the conversation coming from the kitchen. The Americans could not speak German, and our people could not speak English. But laughter and talking we could hear; they had a good time. The men came back several times. That home-baked cake tasted better than their military rations I'm sure, and so many Americans had German ancestors. I believe that many missed that family togetherness. They were still so young and had been away from home for a long time, had seen so many friends die or get wounded. Two soldiers had relatives in our village. One came early on and saw his relatives. The other was stationed farther away and was stopped by his officers when he tried to see them.

That was also the time when I got a sore throat that would not get better. After a week in bed, the Dartmans sent me home. They had work to do in the fields, and I was no help. Mom called the doctor who lived across the street from us. When he checked my throat, he said that I had angina pectoris. By then my limbs were getting stiff and were hurting. He told Mom right in front of me that I would never walk again. That was hard for me to swallow. He prescribed some medicine and an ointment for my joints. Mom packed cotton around my arms and legs. At night she had to get up many times just to move my legs; I did not have the strength to do it myself. Those were difficult times for me. I did not want to be in a wheelchair for the rest of my life. Mom would sit next to my bed, and I wanted to know what kind of funeral she was going to have for me. How we went through this, I don't remember; she would help my grandparents in the field during the day too, and I was alone during the day. The doctor never came back; we could only pay with money. He wanted food, which he got enough from the farmers. He was also a refugee with a wife and two children. I can understand that he wanted food, but he was on the road all day long and doctoring was not all he did during the day. It was rumored that he also took care of lonely widows on his visits.

In the meantime, the soldiers were moved from the lower village to the upper one. My aunt did not have to take anyone; a quarantine sign was posted on her house. She was happy about it, and I did not care. Mom got a doctor for me from the city, Friedrichroda, where I had worked before. It was the daughter of the doctor I had seen with my leg wound. She could only come after office hours and did not make it back in time to be home when curfew started. But she came anyway and did not have any problems; she only had to show her ID. She gave me a different medicine, and my health slowly improved. She visited every week, and after six weeks in bed, I finally was allowed to get up a few minutes a day. When she said five minutes, I stayed up ten and was very wobbly. All I could do was stay at the window and enjoy the sunshine. It was May by now, and everyone was working in the fields. The soldiers across the street hollered when they saw me. "Baby sick?" they asked, and I nodded my head. "Baby chocolate?" My head nodded again, and one of them threw a bar of chocolate up in my window. I saved it till Mom came home that night. I offered her half the bar, but she refused. "That's from our enemies," she said, "the ones that destroyed our homes." That bar tasted so good, but I offered Mom a bite again, and she took it. We had been deprived for so long, she could not resist. The Dartmans had been sending butter and milk for me all through my sickness, which helped some.

Mom had forgotten to close the curtain one morning before she left, and I had gone to sleep with my back to the window. When I awoke and turned around, the guys from across the street could look into our window, hollering; they had been watching me. That went on for two hours until Mom came home from the fields. I did not dare to get up and close the curtain even though I was wearing pajamas; I just pulled the sheet up and turned my back toward the window.

My stay-up time increased, and when I heard a lot of shouting one day, I went to the window. The GIs must have been bored; they did all kind of things that would get the people upset, like blowing up condoms and hanging them out the windows. All the children that walked by wanted a balloon; the mothers had a hard time explaining. When the shepherd returned with the cows in the evening, the guys would try to ride them, which confused the animals; they were not used to that. It resulted in a wild chase through the village with the cows missing the stalls where they were supposed to stop. That got the farmers upset. One of the soldiers who looked more Mexican—his skin was darker and his features a little different—played the banjo on the front steps. He made beautiful music, and it sounded like he was homesick; I enjoyed listening to it. My sister had come by to visit just from the street; she was not allowed in the house yet. A soldier wanted to come inside. He tried all the windows and doors, but everything was locked. I told my sister to get the mayor right away if the guy would make it inside; he would have raped me. The back doors from my aunt's house were open but could only be reached through the backyard, which the soldier did not know. My sister still looked like a small child; he did not bother her. She did babysitting for the children in the bakery, which meant good food. Only she ate very little compared to me.

Finally, the day came when I could stay up for thirty minutes. I had to see the Dartmans; I figured I could make it in twenty minutes. However, I was weaker than I thought; it took me over thirty. I was so exhausted that the two steps leading up to their entrances were too much for me. I just collapsed on the bottom step, and no one opened the door. They were staying inside, had seen me coming, but were so upset about my feeble condition that they cried, and it took them awhile to compose themselves. Now they brought even more food over to get me back to my former self.

Their daughter had come back from the air force while I was gone, and Paul did not need extra help. He told me that I should come back as soon as I was well enough and stay with them until I had my strength back and gained some weight. I did, and my stay with them was about six months. One afternoon, word got around that the Americans exchanged yoyos for two eggs apiece. Renate and my cousin Karen wanted one, and Grandma had to pay with four eggs. I was supposed to go along. Only two soldiers were in a place in the woods; the kids gave them the eggs, and they got the yoyos. As we walked back, one of them shot at us, and we fell flat on the ground. They were drunk and laughed like crazy. They just wanted to scare us, but hitting the ground when hearing shots was a natural thing to do then. Soon after, the soldiers left, their jeeps lined with down comforters and pillows. Radios, silverware, and good china disappeared with them. Not all of them did this, but quite a few of them did. A few days later, the Russians arrived.

That year I also was able to witness the birth of a calf, finally. Renate had done that so many years before; now it was my turn. We had neighbors helping, and it took several hours before the calf was born. I was instructed to hold the tail to one side while Mr. Dartman turned the calf around and pulled the hoofs out. I was not sure if this was something you do for a birth or if Mr. Dartman was just having fun with me. I let go of the tail not because I was not sure, but that cow turned around and looked at me with those large brown eyes like she wanted to say "This hurts like crazy." The men just laughed when I left the cowshed. Everyone got home safely after the delivery, and now came my job: I could teach the calf to drink. The calf was lying on a pile of fresh straw, and I was crouching next to it, putting my finger in its mouth, always wetting my fingers with fresh milk. It caught on pretty fast and was sucking happily on my fingers and later out of the bowl. That was a wonderful experience. Seeing the rabbits being born was different. I was alarmed when I saw all the blood around the female's mouth. I believed she was eating the young, but she was only licking her babies dry. Those rabbits kept meat on the dinner table during Sundays throughout the year. The Dartmans had around sixty rabbits all the time; they multiply so fast. I had never witnessed anything like that before.

THE RUSSIANS ARE COMING

They didn't look as civilized as the Americans; some were riding horses. One of the men in the village was a communist; everyone knew it. He ran toward them with his fist high in the air and screamed, "Welcome, I'm a communist." One Russian just hit him over the head with his bayonet. The Russians looked brutal and mean; their uniforms were dirty. The Americans had been so neat; their uniforms were always freshly washed and pressed. What a difference. The Russians built huts outside the village along the street. It was just a three-sided hut with two shelves inside, where they sleep next to each other with their feet sticking out on the open side of the hut. One always stayed watch, with his rifle over his shoulder. So many of them never slept in beds before, like the prisoner my aunt had to help on her farm. He did not speak German, and she did not speak Russian. The first night, the man slept on the floor. To make him understand that the bed was for sleeping, she opened the cover and lay down on the bed the following night. Of course, she did not undress. When she went to his room the next morning, his bed was dirty; he had slept in it with his clothes and shoes on. Somehow she made him understand that he had to take his clothes off, and the shoes she could demonstrate. Also, she added that he should wash himself. He was a feeble old man and could just sweep the barnyard, feed the chickens, little things like that. He always asked to polish our shoes and would call Mom "Madam." He had to leave when his countrymen came. He cried; he wanted to stay. He never had it so good in his life. We felt the same; we got so used to having him around and felt sorry that he had to go back to Russia. At his age and feeble condition, he probably never made it back to his home. It is strange how things happen in a war. Hitler and the German people were judged by the whole world and made out to be inhuman, and here is this Russian prisoner who loved it there and was never treated as well in his own country.

One sunny day as we were getting fresh grass, a boy from the village came running toward us. He shouted, "The Russians are at your house, they want beer." We scrambled to load the wagon with the grass and hurried home. Only two Russians were at the front door; they watched us girls unload the grass. Holly, Paul's daughter, was a pretty young woman, had a nice bosom and natural blond curls cascading down her back. She was a little on the chubby side and an ideal woman for one of the Russians. At last he said so to her father; he wanted to take her back to Russia with him. "No, no," he said, "take her," pointing to me. I thought I would die of fear, and Mr. Dartman laughed. This went on and on, but finally, the soldiers left to drink the beer, and we all felt safe again.

Another time when making hay, Mom needed a bathroom. Every field had people working, turning the grass so it would dry. She could not crouch behind a bush without being seen. A shot-up railroad train was standing on the tracks, the broken windows covered with wooden planks. Mom thought that would be the perfect place to go in. To her surprise, she noticed that most seats in first and second class had the upholstery cut out. Now she knew where our neighbors across the street had gotten their new winter coats. All the seats had two layers of fabric. First class had a thick white wool fabric, which then was covered with a thick plush fabric. Second class had a light-gray undercover and a red plush fabric on top. She did not tell anyone and decided to get up at three the next morning. She left with a knife and a shopping bag and made it undetected into the railcar. The upholstery in first class was all gone. Second class had red striped plush and a thick gray wool fabric under that—a good quality fabric.

After she had her bag full, she heard a noise and slid under the seat, shaking. She thought the police were after her. The man that came into the car was the neighbor, ready to get more fabric. He did not see her, and she kept still until he left. She scrambled out after him and hurried home. She had enough fabric for a skirt and vest and to make my outgrown winter coat into a jacket. It was not the same fabric, but everybody had clothes that were constructed from two different colors then.

My outfit turned out very well, and we decided that I should learn tailoring, something my home economics teacher had suggested. From the plush fabric, I made house slippers for my family, and since it was close to Christmas, I made slippers for the refugees across the street also. I had befriended the daughter, who was my age and who was sickly. She died shortly thereafter of tuberculosis. I am grateful that God protected me from that illness, but I do test positive when I get tested for TB.

In the spring of 1946, I took another sewing class; and around Easter, I had a job as a tailor's apprentice in Friedrichroda, the town I had worked in before. A Russian commander was a customer; we had to make bras for him. Men can have that much bosom? We never saw him without his uniform. The commanders looked fairly neat in their uniforms with all the medals plastered over their chests. Since we could not purchase much and my mother thought I did not need it, I made patterns from Mom's bra and sewed my own. It made me feel more grown up. Those bras lasted till I was nineteen, when I finally made enough money to buy new ones in a store.

At first I still could take the train to work. When the train whistle sounded at the station, I had to run to make it to the next stop. Most times I was punctual; I would rather be five minutes early than late. (Which I still do today or did all through my life.) But taking the train also meant I was one hour early for work. That was not a problem in the summer; I would sit that hour in the park eating all my sandwiches. My breakfast consisted of fried potatoes, fried in black coffee, which did not satisfy me; I was still hungry. My lunch consisted of ten slices of bread and a cup of cottage cheese. That was gone before I started work. You might think that I was a large size with all the food I consumed, but I only was a size seven. I was lucky though; one of the girls came from the same village. She was even smaller than I was, and her parents always packed a large lunch for her. She often offered me a sandwich, and her parents were happy when she came home with an empty lunch bag. No nagging from her mom that she did not eat enough.

Our food rations under the Russian regime were irregular. Some months there was no meat, and we would get cheese instead. Twenty-four rolls of cheese for a whole month and no refrigerator. Milk and butter we usually purchased every few days fresh if it was available. But all that cheese had to last for a whole month. In the summer, it would be full of worms after two weeks, and we had to feed it to the pigs. Mom would cook farina, chop an onion, brown it, and add some melted fat back, salt, and marjoram, which made a nice sandwich spread. Often we would not have an onion, which made the spread less tasty.

The two girls who lived across the street were my friends. Their father had died in the war, and their mother was running the grocery store by herself. We decided one pretty Sunday night to go to their garden cottage and try out some whisky that had come in that day. The whisky was stored in a large wooden barrel, and I watched speechless as they took a pint of whisky out of the barrel and replaced it with a pint of water. We had a good time tasting the whiskey that evening, but on the way home, I was not so steady on my feet and decided that I would not drink alcohol anymore. Mom never found out; she thought I was safe when I went out with girls. But we would always have a glass of wine with the special holiday dinners at home or in a restaurant later, when everything was available again.

The Russians dismantled the train tracks and sent them east. We thought they were sent to Russia, but twenty years later, piles of tracks were found in Poland; my sister saw them when she went there to see the home of her husband's parents, who had to flee when the Russians came. Helmut was taken to Siberia at age ten and was released from prison camp ten years later when he was too sick to work. His parents did not recognize him when he came back from Russia. His whole body was swollen from fluids. All the men that had been in Siberia came back sick with kidney problems, or their bodies were emancipated.

Now we had to walk to work, which took about one hour. This was no problem in the summer; but to walk for an hour when it was so bitter cold outside was no fun. Our eyelashes would be covered with ice. Every little facial hair was looking white. We wore shawls over our mouths to keep the cold wind out. And we always walked in a large group with older men from the village that worked in Friedrichroda and also with the younger folks of all ages. That's why the Russians never bothered us; we were in the majority. They had raped one sixty-two-year-old woman, stuffed grass thatches in her mouth and ears, and tied her skirts together over her head. Four of them did that; the woman was so damaged that she had to be in the hospital for two years. I still think it was a miracle that none of us were ever molested. The Russian army commanders had promised their soldiers that they could rape every woman in Germany. And in the large cities, they did; it was horrible. There was a time, many years later, that I got real angry that Mom let me go to work at that time, when I realized how much danger we had been in. But I probably would do it again. You can't hide; you can only hope and pray that you will be safe.

I did miss the park sometimes, the azaleas in particular. When I sat there, it felt like I was on holiday. The benches were surrounded by flowers and other blooming bushes and trees. God had dressed nature in his Sunday best. The yellow azaleas had a special intoxicating scent. I'm always looking for that special one and can't find it here. Maybe our spring here is too hot for these plants. The name of the park used to be Hermann Göring Park, after the Reichs marshal, but the name was changed as soon as the war was over, like so many streets that were named after the Nazi politicians. I enjoyed my place of work. Five girls were learning a trade, and since I was the youngest, I also had to clean the apartment on weekends. It was against the law, but no one said anything. We were glad to have a place to learn a trade; life was supposed to get better later. Customers had to change in our atelier for the fittings in the winter. (Coal was not available.) I had not seen other people in their underwear, and I started snickering, suppressing my laugh. It embarrassed me when they started undressing. My boss wrote a letter to my mother, and of course, I stopped after the talking to I got. But it took some effort; I guess teenagers giggle everywhere in all countries.

Fridays we had eight hours of schooling where we learned the business side of our profession. The sad part was that all the teachers who had been in the Nazi Party had lost their jobs in the Russian sector. People that previously had not passed the teacher's exam were hired. They also used tailors to instruct us. They knew their business, and we learned something. But the young teacher we had was also dating students, which was a distraction for us. We watched as they shared secret glances and touches in class. It was very funny for us sixteen-year-olds, and it gave us a reason to giggle again. In West Germany, the teachers were denazified, trained in classes to rid themselves of the Nazi influences, and rehired as teachers. The Russians fired everyone and hired people that could not pass the teacher's exams before. The result was that sometimes the students knew more than the teachers. It happened in my math class, and the teacher would just say, "We talk about it next week." So school was boring for me. I remember my sixteenth birthday that year when I had to clean two hundred pounds of sugar beets that my boss was lucky to get to make syrup for sandwiches. It was a rainy day; the water was leaking through the roof, and my back was wet. My hands were ice cold working with the beets all day; I was not a happy camper. It was also bad to have to carry the rugs down three flights of stairs to beat the dust off them. They were so heavy and very bulky to carry all the way down into the backyard.

My father had been released from the military in the meantime. He had been captured by the British after coming from Russia, where he had been all through the war, and he returned to our hometown. He came for a two-week visit and took me with him when he returned. He also took a friend of mine who had a fiancé in Hamburg. This was my vacation. One morning, we left by train to ride to the town that was closest to the border. The wall went up many years later to stop people from leaving. I don't remember the name of the town anymore, but when we descended the train, the platform was full of Russians. They knew already that every train brought people who wanted to go to West Germany. We had to walk to an estate that was close by and had to line up, first the men then the women followed behind them. They controlled our passports, and we were asked questions. Those I don't remember, and I could not hear what they asked my father. I only saw that the interrogator slapped my father in the face. Pop did not feel any goodwill toward them, and he probably said something demeaning in Russian to them. He was not very cooperative, and that scared me. I started running away as fast as I could. Why? I ask myself today. They had guns; what was I thinking? What could my father do? He had to follow his daughter, and my friend followed suit. I ran behind a row of houses and finally saw a raised flower bed and lay flat behind it. My father dropped behind it too, and so did my friend. One Russian followed, with his rifle in front of him. He glanced sideways and noticed us. The three of us had to march back with him. We had to go into the garage at the estate, where the other people were waiting.

The men had to go into the large house and start cleaning it. We women had to wait about two hours before the men were back, and then it was our turn to go inside. My friend Else and I were assigned to wash windows downstairs, something the soldiers knew something about, because we were given vinegar and newspapers. When you dry the windows with newspaper, they won't streak. The whole downstairs windows had to be cleaned, at least twelve, and the soldiers checked for streaks. A commander was coming the next day, and everything was supposed to be sparkling clean. After we finished with the windows, we had to do the bathrooms. I have never seen anything as dirty. The bathtub was one with legs, standing in mud so deep that we had to use a shovel to get rid of the dirt. Also, the inside of the tub was dirty; we scrubbed and scrubbed, but a fine gray film was still present after we finished.

The same with the toilet; dirt was everywhere. Else was not as scared as I was; she asked questions. They had washed potatoes in the toilet bowl and were surprised when they flushed that the potatoes disappeared and the bowl got stuck. The bathtub was not used for taking a bath; they washed their boots in it. That's why there was so much dirt. And when we talked to my dad later, he told us that he had shoveled the dirt out of the bathroom too. But typical of him, he only did it in front of the tub, not behind it. After we had the downstairs done, we were supposed to do the upstairs, washing all the floors. Those floors were bare wood, and Else said, "No way, we are just going to spread the water around so it looks like we cleaned it." Again, I alone would never have dared to do that. Else was five years my senior and not as afraid as I was. Now we filled up the bucket and spread the water all over the floors so they would look wet. We had to do that several times before we walked downstairs where a soldier stood, his rifle pointed at us.

The Russians were always running around with their rifles; not so with the Americans. He told Else that he was going to sleep with her, and she told him no way; her husband was waiting for her. The talk went back and forth for a while, and then he let us go back to the garage, where we

were told to go home. We walked down a field toward the border to West
Germany. One of the soldiers that had arrested us before caught up with
us and told us to go back to East Germany. Pop said, "West Germany is
my home. Look at those people coming over there. Take them and let us
go." And he did; it was that easy. I guess it is easier to be nice to them than
show fear. They can see it in your eyes, and it encourages them to take
advantage of you. It was getting dark now, and we hurried down the field
and crouched behind some bushes until the moon came out. My father
knew the way; we walked for hours, and then finally, there is a railroad
station. And we realized that was the West.

It's only a two-hour train ride, and we are in Braunschweig, my
hometown. I cried; I didn't know where I was. Three years ago, I had left
my hometown, and now I was lost. I didn't recognize the streets; everything
was in rubble. Before we were evacuated in the fall of 1943, we had about
284 hours of air raids. Now, after the war, we were told the total was 1,073
air raids during the whole war; and this was only on our city. The dead
numbered 2,905. Our city had fewer deaths because we had more bunkers
for people to go to. If I had not known which way the trams were going, I
would have been lost. Ruins were everywhere, street after street after street.
Our apartment house was still standing, surrounded by a sea of destruction.
It was nice to walk inside, to see our furniture. My mother's sister and her
husband lived in our living room; they had lost everything during an air
raid. My father lived in our bedroom, and the kitchen was shared by all.
Some people lived in basements that are temporarily patched up. And still,
I was happy to be home. Most families had only one room to live in after
the war.

My aunt worked in a restaurant outside the city. The other place near
the theater where she had worked before had been bombed also. It took us
over one hour to walk there. It was the place we had visited so often years
before on our Sunday outings. Aunt Luise worked in the kitchen as a cook.

I went to the kitchen and stood at the door; customers were not allowed in there. Nobody said anything, and my aunt glanced over at me several times and did not recognize me. I had left when I was thirteen, and now I was sixteen. My hair was short, not in pigtails anymore; I looked like a young woman. I could not take the suspense any longer and just walked into the kitchen and gave her a hug. She served us a big dinner that night for which we did not have to pay. She had done this years ago too, when she waited tables and had a good day with lots of tips. We had so much to talk about when we all got home. The two weeks passed pretty fast; I located some friends and tried to find my way around the city. My father took me to some of his customers whose hair he cut in the evenings. One of them had a grocery store. He asked the owner if he had some candy for his daughter, but he did not give me any. That was a very embarrassing moment for me. First I was hopeful, and then I felt ashamed that my father had begged. I was lucky to have nice weather for my stay. My green skirt and the white blouse I had made out of two pillowcases looked nice with my suntan. (Pillowcases in Germany are more than twice the size of the ones we have here in the States.)

My friend Else joined us again on the way back to East Germany. We had no problems crossing the border safely into the Russian zone, which we did during the night. You could hear dogs howling in the distance, meaning the patrols were still far away. After our return, my family started planning our trip back to the West, which took another year. Just crossing the border would not have been too hard, but we had taken furniture with us when we left. To transport them at night across the border going back was harder to arrange. People were killed after hiring guides to cross the border; many were robbed. It was a scary time.

The musicians in our village started practicing in the doll factory again. Dancing had been forbidden the last years of the war. All the younger single people were taught by the older ones how to dance. Dancing came easy for me, and I enjoyed it very much. I still like it today but get out of breath doing it. I just loved dancing the waltz or the tango. The polka was great too; I felt alive dancing around the ballroom. It was nice to be young and full of energy. It did not take long, and we had the first ball. Now I needed a new dress, something special. But where to get the fabric? The stores were empty. It was easier for the farmers; they could get anything from the people in the city for food. A lot of bartering was going on between those people. We were not so lucky and had to make do with what we had. That meant out of two, make one. My dress was black with a red top. Mom had a black coat with a satin lining. We took the lining out, which was enough for the skirt; and for the top, we used her red slip from her blue Swiss-embroidery dress. She just wore a regular slip under her dress from then on. My dress was perfect, and I called it my lucky dress because every time I wore it, I would dance every dance. I learned that the long dress was not as important; no one really cared if the dress was long or short for the first ball. That we were healthy and could dance was the important thing. I had that dress for many years and always felt very special in it.

I also joined the choir. Everyone from fourteen to sixty was singing. All those people had the same teachers over the years and all knew the same folk songs. We would perform on special occasions in our village and other villages. Sometimes when there was a dance in any of the villages close by, the Russians would come and control our passports. That was always scary. They never came alone, always in a larger group and always with rifles over their shoulders. None ever spoke German; an interpreter would accompany them. That disrupted everything; we felt threatened and we did not dare to be uncooperative. After the inspection, they would sit on the stage at a long table that had to be provided in a hurry. They would pick one girl or several, depending on how many men had come. The girls had to join them on the stage. One time an interpreter asked me to dance with him and invited me to sit on the stage with them. I excused myself, told him I had to freshen up in the bathroom, and ran home. The boys from our school were nice; they would walk us girls home. It made us feel safer to have them walk with us. The interpreter had been at least thirty; I would not have felt safe with him. They had been drinking too, another reason for me to disappear.

One time, I witnessed a Russian taking a bike away from a little boy. It was an old rusty bike he was riding down the street, his hands high in the air. A Russian was standing there with a new bike, and he can't ride it. He takes the old bike away from the boy and gives him the new one in the hope that he can ride the old one as well as the boy. He was not so lucky, and the smart little guy had disappeared in the meantime. Such things happened. Also, taking out the light switch plates from the walls, in the hope it would give them electricity back in Russia. Those must have been the troops from the backlands that never had electricity before. Those happenings brought some laughter into our lives. Our neighbor across the street had something similar happen to him. He borrowed an old bike from the farmer next door to ride to the city for something official he had to do; I do not recall what. He saw a Russian lean his new bike against the wall of an office building, and as soon as the Russian had disappeared inside, he took the new bike and left his old one and pedaled home as fast as he could. The farmer was happy to get a new bike in return.

The only men I trusted were Mr. Bemmel, who owned the grocery store, and the meat inspector. Mr. Bemmel had to drive to Friedrichroda once a month to deliver the ration cards; and the meat inspector, who also had a motorcycle, had to make the same trip. When I heard their motorcycles on the way home from work, I would stop walking. They would let me ride on the backseat. The meat inspector was younger, and I loved the way he drove through a curve, leaning to one side. None of the other girls would do that, and neither would the boys.

Another time I was reckless; a car passed and the man asked me if he could take me home. I agreed; I thought since he had to pass my house, nothing bad could happen. After a while, he put his hand on my knee, which I brushed off. When I told him to stop, he drove past my house. I got a little panicky then; my right hand had already opened the door and I would have jumped out, but he finally stopped. Needless to say, I never did that again, and I never told Mom either.

The winter of 1946 was very cold with snow piled up high on the side of the highways and stayed there for several weeks. Walking home three miles in that cold weather was no fun. Sometimes I took my skis; other times when I had to deliver the dresses to the customers, I took the sled. That would be on a Saturday, and since the town where I worked was hilly, the sled could transport me faster. There were not many people on the street on a cold Saturday morning, so I could ride the sled on the sidewalk. When I held on to the back of a slow-moving truck going my way, everybody hollered, "Don't do that, it's too dangerous." It was fun for a while sliding over the snow and passing everyone on the way home. But then I spotted the bridge ahead, which would not have snow under it. So I threw my purse forward, which slid nicely into the snowbank, and then I let myself go. I did the same thing, sliding very fast over the street into that pile of snow. It just hurt a little as I made contact with the ground, but I never repeated that again either. I had worked a lot already in my short life and had so many responsibilities that I had to do something crazy, I think. Whoever reads this, please don't try it. I was very lucky to get away without any serious injury.

We also had the first fashion show that year, a very special event for me. All the tailors in the city made it happen in the hotel downtown. I knew a customer would bring the dress we had made for her daughter, a lovely light-blue lace dress for her first dance. I was hoping against all hope that I could wear it at the show. It was not that I wanted to prance around in front of all the people; I just wanted to wear that beautiful dress for just a little while, to feel well-off and rich like its owner. I fixed my hair real pretty that day, wore the high-heeled shoes my aunt had given me. They were a little too short but were my first high heels, so I squeezed my feet into them. I wore my best silk stockings to work that day. We did not have nylons then, and since we could not buy new stockings, we had to mend the old ones. I was lucky that I had a pair where the mending did not show. The holes in the toes had been darned with yarn from our sofa pillow. Its large multicolored tassel got a lot thinner over the years before we could buy darning yarn again. And it did happen; the customer brought her daughter's dress and asked my boss if I could model it. She hated for other strangers to wear it. Fortunately, I was the same size as her daughter. I was elated and was rushed to the backstage. The show had already started, and as soon as I got backstage, they dressed me in a navy suit with a white trim around the lapels. Under it I wore a white blouse, and to top it all off, I had to wear the prettiest navy hat with large white flowers under the rim in the back. I looked really nice and a lot more mature. The runway seemed awful long. I thought I would never be able to go to the end and return; my knees felt like rubber. Mom had the best seat in the room, right at the end of the runway. As I walked toward it, she said fairly loud and surprised, "That is Sigrid." I smiled my way through it. Later I was modeling that pretty lace dress. That was a big event in my life. If I had told Mom in advance that she needed the camera that night, she would have laughed and said I was crazy. It was a fairy tale evening for me.

A new mayor was installed in our village after the Russians had come; he was a communist and had been in the concentration camp some time during Hitler's reign. We had tried several times over the last two years to get a certificate for a new pair of shoes for me. I got really upset one day; I thought Mom might not be firm enough, so I decided to confront the mayor and plead for a certificate myself. It was a warm summer day, and his windows were open wide. He said again as he had done so many times before, "Your ration cards have been lost. I can't give you another one." I told him then that he had used our cards for his family. They were wearing new dresses and shoes all the time. He did get loud; he screamed at me that it was not true. He called me all kinds of names, and I answered in a calm voice. I did not get a certificate for a pair of shoes, but lots of people in the village knew what I had done. As I left his office, a crowd had gathered under the window outside; they wanted to see who got him so upset.

Now it was time to arrange for our trip home. The trucking firm had agreed to get our furniture. All we had to do was find someone in East Germany to transport them to the border for us. We were lucky and found someone fairly soon that would transport the furniture to the border and help unload and reload them. It all happened without incident, and then we left during the night. But in the morning, we were in West Germany in a refugee camp. We received medical checkups, new legal papers for reentry to the West, and after a delousing spray, we were able to go. Not that we had any lice, but there were so many others that had been traveling for weeks, people who had to sleep in barns or on the side of the road. It was mandatory to be sprayed.

We were six people living in our apartment now, which was difficult after a while. My aunt and uncle got permission to make an apartment out of the room where we used to dry our clothes. It was next to the laundry room, where we had to take turns with the other people in our apartment house to wash our laundry every six weeks. The laundry room was quite large with a large copper kettle where we would boil our white linens, and Mom would follow up washing everything by hand in large wooden tubs. Three days she would stay in there and do our wash. She never asked me to help, and I was so glad that she didn't. I would help with hanging up the clothes on the clothesline and with the ironing later. In the summer, we hung the clothes outside, and on rainy days inside a room where my aunt and uncle now had permission to make an apartment for themselves. Hanging up clothes was an art too; everything had to be hung just so: sheets and pillowcases together, then towels, washcloths, and dish towels. In between we would hide the undergarments; those were too private. The best tablecloth would hang on the outside so people could see that you had beautiful things. Mom had two half aprons with a large pocket for the clothespins. We tied them around our waist when hanging up the laundry. They had been embroidered by hand, with blue embroidery thread, Mom's favorite color.

When we had a few things that had to be washed by hand, we could hang them out the windows. But we could only use the windows that pointed away from the street; and only till eleven in the morning. After that time, everything had to look neat. The same with our feather beds. We would air them in the windows once a week. In a large city, you have to have rules like that, or it would look like slums in no time. You would always know when you were in Germany; it looked neater than any other European country.

1947—WE'RE BACK HOME

We were back home. For one and a half years, I had been an apprentice in East Germany. My father had found a place for me in my hometown, which had been filled in the meantime because of our delay with our move. I was lucky and found something fast. He was a tailor who made women's clothing and had seven girls and one tailor working for him. At the time, people who wanted something special would have their clothes made by a tailor, for slowly fabrics had become available again, if one had enough money or could trade on the black market. We could also buy fashion magazines with the newest styles.

I had no problem adjusting to the new workplace; I could keep up with the other people. The only problem was my boss. He made me feel uncomfortable; he had a funny way of looking at me. One morning, I was the first to arrive in the atelier; he cornered me and wanted to kiss me. I pushed him away, and I breathed a sigh of relief when some of the others walked into the room. He tried one more time when his wife was not in the house. We always had to account for each roll of thread, which was still hard to get at the time. He kept this special commodity in a box in his apartment. Certain colors of thread were still scarce in 1947, so we had to be frugal. He also kept a record of how many spools we had used for each outfit. When I had to get some, he asked me a lot of questions about my work, and as he came closer to me, he grabbed my head and held it tight.

As his mouth came closer to mine, I gave him a hard push, which made him tumble backward. I ran as fast as I could and told the girls upstairs. They were not surprised; they just laughed. He had tried this with every one of them and even with customers. After this incident, I always waited in the mornings till one of the others arrived so we could go upstairs together. He died two years later of cancer at age sixty-four. He had not belonged to the ladies' tailor guild; as a consequence, all his apprentices would never get an A for the outfit they had to make as a journeyman. We all ended up with a B, which was not fair. Men at the time hated to follow women's rules and regulations in the guild. But we were innocent and should not have been punished with a lower grade for the way he behaved.

School was difficult for me because the other students were ahead with their curriculum. Now I had to suffer the indignity for being less educated. The communist school system had been inadequate in the beginning. Nobody asked what I had done in the school in East Germany and how well I did. With all these city girls, some two and more years older, I felt like a country bumpkin. It served me right. Our city schools were ahead by a year compared to the country schools, and while we were evacuated, I knew I was ahead of everyone and prided myself about being advanced. Now I paid the price; I was behind in this class. All the school children had been evacuated. The ones who had no relatives in the country had been sent to villages closer to my hometown. They were the first ones who returned to the city and had the benefit of having the old teachers back, the ones that had experience.

Books were not available for us students after the war. The prisoners of war were housed in schools before they were sent back to their countries. They used the books and all the other papers and documents for toilet paper, or they tore them to shreds and hurled them out the windows like confetti. The bookstores and paper factories were all bombed. Paper was scarce and of pure quality right after the war. The main objective was rebuilding houses for the people and rebuilding the factories, not printing books. The students had to write everything down in their notebooks. Now I had to borrow their books and copy everything from the eighteen months I had missed and still keep up with the new curriculum. Practically I had to catch up and do in one and a half years what the others had time to do in three years. That meant I had to study almost every night after work.

A friend of mine came one day and invited me to go to a dance with her. I felt I should do my homework, but Mom talked me into going. She said, "You can't always just sit and study." It was December 18, 1947. That was the day I first met my future husband, Walter. (My second son was born on that day twelve years later.) At the time, I was not interested in dating; I wanted to finish my apprenticeship first. I had done some dating in Oma's village when we were evacuated; but it was just like meeting friends, my school buddies, except for one really nice guy who really loved me. He wrote letters every week. He lived in another village, fifteen miles away. He invited me to the fireman's ball, and I told him I could not go. I knew my mother would never let me go and come back early in the morning. So I never asked her. He also had come back from the war and was twenty-four years old, eight years my senior. He did ask me to marry him; I declined. I wanted to learn a profession first. My mother found those letters one day and was shocked.

In every letter to Helmut, I had said my mother would not let me go to his village because I had to be home by eleven, but that was really not so. It was funny in a way. Mom would always watch behind the window when I came home from a dance. She was always watching me. My cousin had to marry at sixteen because she was pregnant. I remember the teasing I had to endure from the other children in school. My mother told me "Never come home in a condition like that." So I made up my own rules to be home early, and I had no problem with my school buddies; they respected me. If only Mom had told me how a girl came into that predicament. I was thirteen at the time and knew nothing about the birds and the bees. She would always say, "I will tell you when you get married." She did that when I first menstruated too; I was so scared then. Mom did have three stepmothers, so no one explained anything to her. Subjects like those were taboo at the time. It's something I decided to do different when I had children, and that turned out a lot different from what I expected.

I was relieved when my boys did not ask any questions. They were seven and ten when a friend gave me a nice book that explained how babies grew in a mother's tummy. The boys read it, and Tom said nothing. Roger had a completely different reaction, which we had not expected. He glanced through the book and told me that he would never believe a story like that—to grow from a small seed, no way. And I was a coward after all; I did not correct him. So I did not do so well either. And my husband avoided the subject altogether.

I did meet my future husband that first night when I went to that dance. I enjoyed dancing with him, and he was pretty persistent; he came to every dance. By eleven, I was home again and went back the next Sunday to the same place. He was there again, and we mostly danced with each other. After the fourth time, I let him bring me home. This continued till March 7, my birthday. He came to our home and surprised me with a present, a book and a fountain pen. Now I had to ask him in and introduce him to my parents. The funny thing was that he was my father's customer. Walter had been in the war. He had been drafted out of school at age sixteen. He was on the eastern front and received a head injury. He always said he should not have raised his head after the Russians had stopped shooting. He wanted to see where the shooting came from. He was lucky; the wound was between his nose and eye. Since later tests could not find any metal splinters in his head, it was assumed that a stone hit his face and caused the injury. He was lucky and was shipped out before the Russians took over the territory. The other ship that followed later with other refugees was torpedoed and sank. He was also in Holland, where he was shot through his hand by a British soldier earlier.

He was captured by the Americans when the war was over. Since he was born in Mahanoy City in Pennsylvania, they wanted to send him back to the States right away. He explained that he wanted to see his parents first and see if they were still alive. His parents were living in Burg, close to Magdeburg in the Russian sector. They were making plans to go to West Germany; the Russians knew that his father was an American citizen and told him to leave. Their destination was Brunswick, my hometown. They had encountered the same problem with their move to West Germany as we had. Walter was learning a trade as a radio mechanic then. When he learned that we did not have a radio, he built us one. His school sold refreshments like chocolate milk and small cans of Del Monte Fruit Cocktail. This was shipped over by the Americans. He shared that fruit cocktail with me. I thought that was so generous, seeing how skinny he was. He joined me on my swim team but eventually stopped going. He was not the sporty type, and I stopped after a while too.

Since I was now eighteen, I took dancing lessons. It was the custom to do that between sixteen and eighteen years of age, not just to learn the proper ballroom dancing, but also to learn proper etiquette. I was in my element, loved every minute of it, especially when the girls could ask the men for a dance. I was the first one who asked the instructor to dance. That was the best dance I ever danced in my life, just perfect. It did not last long enough for me; I could have gone on forever. The other girls wanted to dance with the instructor too, so I had to give him up. I would wait impatiently for the next week to arrive to be able to go dancing again.

My studies continued, and it was time to order fabric for the outfit I had to make for my journeyman's diploma. The stores did not have nice-enough fabrics yet. One small store owner went to the French border where he could get good quality wool fabrics. He had to drive to the border to pick up the fabric himself. I ordered three yards of a light-blue wool fabric to make a skirt and a jacket. The fabric cost me 108 marks. I made 47 marks a month and had to give my mother 15 marks for food. It took me a long time to save that money. I hardly ever rode the tram to work or on Sundays when we would go to the park. We walked everywhere. On Sundays, we would average easily ten miles of walking. I got the fabric early enough and had time to design my dress. Students were judged on several things. The color of the fabric had to compliment one's skin color. The pattern and style of the dress had to be right for our figures and had to have a few special touches of workmanship on it. I could not go wrong with my fabric selection; light blue was my color. I designed a flared skirt, which always makes a nice figure.

By then the styles had changed; the skirts were worn down to the lower calf. The jacket was tight fitting with a shawl collar and had a flared coattail and long sleeves with real buttonholes. When I say real buttonholes, I mean bound buttonholes. I decorated the left side of the jacket with a black velvet application and embroidery. I had only one week to finish not only the dress but also a special piece of cloth that had to have all the special details, seams, and pockets we had learned and done over the past three years on it.

My work turned out nice; I was pleased and scared at the same time. You never knew what the other girls would make or what the judges liked. My boss thought it was excellent workmanship. We had to make the outfit at another tailor's shop so no one could or would cheat, and we had exactly forty hours to finish our work. The written test came a week later. For that test, we had to pick several subjects out of a hat, and lucky for me, it was something I had copied just the week before and remembered everything verbatim. How nice that is to remember everything. Today, in 2011, only the past is easy to remember; everything else is forgotten or takes days before I remember.

We had to wait for the test results outside the school building. It made me feel queasy in my stomach, and I was glad when the waiting was over. I had done well and received my journeyman's certificate. I dreamed of this day several times for the following twenty years. Looking back, it must have been a lot of pressure for studying this all in eighteen months. My boss was happy too and told me that I had a job in his firm. A few weeks later, he died of cancer, and four weeks after that, his wife closed the shop. She said that she did not have any money, so I had worked the last week for nothing. We were promised to get paid later, but she never did. She reopened later with fewer people. When I applied many years later for a job in the United States, she was the only one that did not reply when questions were asked if I had been employed in her shop.

When our milkman noticed me during the day in his store, he was curious and asked why I was home. I told him my situation, and he hired me instantly to make several dresses for his wife. She had a sewing machine, so I could do all the sewing in her apartment. That saved a lot of time. I had my customer there and did not have to wait for her to come for the fittings. She served wonderful meals, and I made considerably more money. I could accomplish so much more. After doing this for four weeks, Mom thought that was enough. Her thought was that it was shameful not to be employed at a business. I had to look for another job and was hired right away by the largest department store in our city. Now I had a respectable job, and Mom was happy.

Twelve ladies worked in the women's alterations department. But I felt like a stranger in there. Everyone was older, and I could feel the difference of having lived in a village for four years. I had an inferiority complex; I was not as sophisticated as these city girls. A few weeks, later a position opened up in the men's department. Four tailors worked there and twenty ladies did alterations or made new coats. I applied for the position and was transferred with a nice raise in my salary. What a wonderful change that was. Half of the ladies were my age, and we all formed nice relationships with each other. We are still friends today as I write this all down, over sixty years later. Only one has died in the meantime.

We all got engaged and married. We all had the same upbringing, and everyone was happy when we could purchase something. We would go shopping together and found fun in little things. Even buying an orange was something special then. Each orange cost fifty cents, which we could not afford every day, not even once a week. What a marvelous fruit to hold in your hand. When one of us needed shoes, at least four would go along and enjoy the experience. My mom had gone with me before, and all I got were practical shoes. Now I went with my friends and I had stylish shoes, but Mom's feelings were hurt.

One in our group got married, and we were all invited to the *Polterabend*. On a *Polterabend*, friends bring old dishes and break them in front of the house. The fragments of the broken dishes have to be swept up by the groom later. This is supposed to bring good luck. Only one girl had a boyfriend with a car, a Volkswagen. How do you squeeze eight people into a bug? The driver was on the left, and I sat in the front with a girl on my lap. Four were sitting in the backseat, and the smallest was scrunched up in the luggage compartment. We had to duck several times to hide from the police car that was passing us. It was against the law to have a car overloaded. If you have ever driven in a Volkswagen Bug, you know it is almost impossible; but when you are young and desperate and skinny, it works just fine, and it was fun. We had a wonderful evening with lots of good food. That couple immigrated to Australia. Another of my colleagues moved to Chicago, which I was able to visit many years later too. What a sight to fly into that city at night. All those lights, it was a special treat. The radio had German programs all day. I thought I was in Germany when I saw all the German stores, all the goodies from times past.

Sometimes people throw the dishes in front of city hall. When someone has lots of friends and colleagues, a lot of dishes accumulate, and the groom has a lot of cleaning up to do. If an innocent young girl approaches him and gives him a kiss, he is allowed to stop sweeping. The grooms usually don't wait for a girl to come to them because most girls run the other way. So as soon as he sees a girl, he approaches her and asks politely for a kiss. When all this is going on, the family provides a lot of champagne, and everyone is in a happy mood. Max, my cousin's son, did it that way; and we enjoyed the evening a lot. But that happened many years later when we were already living in the United States.

At night after work, I would do a lot of sewing for friends and relatives. And at Easter, a time when most people got a new outfit, we took work home. Good Friday was a holiday, and I worked at least sixteen hours those Fridays. We got paid extra, and we all were happy. We started to work for our hope chest. We really did not have hope chests like we have here, but we saved things for the future, for the time we would get married.

Carnival starts November 11, and from November till Ash Wednesday, we had masquerade dances. We might attend one or two and enjoyed all of them. I had a snowflake costume once; one time I wore a Hungarian outfit. I especially liked the red boots that came with it. When I wore a gipsy outfit, I won second prize, which was a carton of cigarettes. My other costumes were powder puff and cat. I felt really glamorous when I made a princess costume. Sometimes you needed a lot of imagination to guess what the costume represented. We always made our own costumes to save money. My parents would go to one of those parties with their friends also. That did not stop Mom from checking on me. One time she had to walk fifty minutes in the dark to the place where we celebrated. It hurt that she did not trust me.

On one of my birthdays, I took doughnuts to an afternoon dance. Since Mom had no oil to fry them in, she used castor oil. I did not tell our friends about that. I was a little apprehensive—no, not a little, I was very much afraid that there might be an unwelcome reaction. Nothing happened; no one could taste the castor oil at all. We did a lot of things simply because we had to. That was four years after the war; times were not back to normal then.

Renate was too little to start her apprenticeship as a beautician; she went to school for another year. After she recuperated from a serious kidney infection, she started to eat and to grow several inches, though she stayed always a petite person, a size four when she got married. As a beautician, she was unbeatable. The beauticians would have a contest every year for the best-done hairstyles. Renate would choose me as her model; that was always a nice event. That happened before and after I was married. I was wearing a hairdo for a bride with a little crown in my hair. I looked better at that contest than on my own wedding day. I made our dresses, and Renate did our hairdos; we always looked nice. But dresses take so much longer to make. I never had much leisure time, and Walter would sit many times next to me at the sewing machine. Most dates consisted of going to the park on Sundays and maybe having a cup of coffee and a piece of torte, or dancing at night.

Birthdays were always celebrated with family and friends and with lots of homemade cakes.

ENGAGED

Walter proposed and I accepted. We had been dating for two years. The party was at my house. It was just a small party with dinner and then coffee and cake after. Walter's uncle Frank (his mother's brother) with his wife came from Hannover, about one hour's train ride away. Hannover is also the capital of Lower Saxony.

When we were getting the small gold ring, his father suggested not to put our initials in the ring, as is the custom in Germany. In case the engagement would break up, Walter could use the ring again, he tells him in front of me! In Germany, the couples wear the small gold ring on their left hand when they get engaged. When they get married, the ring is worn on the right ring finger. My engagement present was a wristwatch, my first watch. His mother's comment was, "I should get that, I'm his mother." If she did not have one, I could maybe feel some sympathy, but she had three watches. I wanted to say something, but Mom stopped me. I thought it would be better to clear the air, but—as usual—I do what Mom wants. Now they want me to call them Mom and Dad. It is hard to say the words; they don't act like parents; *rivals* seems the correct word. My other thought was, after they knew me better, they were going to like me. But it had been already two years; how long did they need? She had formerly made fun of my shoes in front of her friend. It took a long time, a very long time with the father, and with her, never. My father would go to the pub every day and guzzle beer and play cards. Walter's father was a good provider but so bossy, he made all the decisions. He and Uncle Frank purchased new suits, and now they were arguing whose was the better one. I hope against hope that they wouldn't ask me. Finally, the dreaded question was asked. Should I be honest or should I lie? "Please tell us, you are the expert, I hear." But only till they hear my answer. I would explain that a tightly woven thread makes a superior fabric, and Uncle Frank's suit was made with that thread. Now my dear father-in-law decided that I have no idea what I'm talking about. I have one friend left, Uncle Frank. When I made myself a dress or bought shoes, my mother-in-law bought the same fabric and shoes. And then I had to make her a dress. Make her stuff first, my mother said; I could wait. Make her happy. I think it is wrong, but I do what Mom wants.

One terrible night, my father came home late; he argued with my mother and raised his hand. I was afraid he was going to hit her and told him, "Stop, don't hit Mom." And now his anger turned toward me, and he hit me in my face, one blow after the other. I didn't sleep much that night. I was contemplating on what to do to him. But I knew I would have to pay a price, and it would be wrong. In the morning, my face was swollen, black and blue. I wore sunglasses for two weeks, and I slept for three nights at Walter's place. I couldn't look at my father. Walter's parents reluctantly let me stay. That's the time when I earnestly thought of going to the United States with Walter. I had expected Mom to come to my aid, and she did not, which hurt. We never talked about the incident. We never talked about our feelings; it would have been better if we had. I suggested to Mom that I would take care of her if she would get a divorce and that I would not immigrate to the United States. She never answered.

Finally, I saved enough money to purchase a bicycle for 240 marks, a lot of money. Now I could ride my bike to work. Most people rode bikes at that time. We had bicycle trails all through the city. And when vacation started, we made a weeklong tour to the Weser River. It was cold and rainy when we left. Another couple was going with us; we rode about forty miles the first day. I was not used to it and was always last. Marge's grandmother lived a little out of the way, but we stayed there overnight, and I remember the delicious lentil soup she had cooked with freshly made blood sausages. In 2009, I took a cruise and heard someone speak German. I talked to that lady and learned that her husband came from the same village where my friend's grandmother had lived, and she came from Hannover, one hour's train ride away from my hometown. It was as if I had met an old neighbor. It really is a small world.

The next day, we made it to the youth hostel where an overnight stay would cost only five marks. But we had to bring our own sheets and pillows. A kitchen was available to cook oatmeal or eggs. Boys slept in one wing and the girls in another. Washrooms were available, and soon after breakfast, we left and kept on traveling. The countryside was very picturesque. We took a boat ride on the Weser River and were lucky to have wonderful weather. We visited a castle in Goslar, and we slept in a tent. Walter wanted to sleep in the woods one night, and we reluctantly agreed, seeing that small tent. As Marge and I cleaned up in the Weser River, the men put up the tent in the woods. Along came a beautiful car with some handsome guys who asked us to come along. We declined but were afraid to go up into the woods. We were afraid that they would follow us. A couple had just been killed in a tent the week before in Holland. When we were sure those men would not come back, we went into the woods and disappeared into the tent. Walter covered our bikes and the tent with leaves. You could only see it when you stood right in front of it. For a while we talked, and as sleep was overtaking us, we heard a noise. Someone was walking outside; the leaves rustled. We stayed real quiet, our hearts beating faster. For a while it was quiet, and then it started again. After the noise stopped, the men fell asleep, but Marge and I did not sleep all night. At least I lay down, but she sat up all night, breathing heavily. The guys went early to the river to wash up and cook breakfast, and then it started again. I think they felt relieved too when they saw what had made that noise during the night. It was deer, lots of them, that went down to the river to drink. We all had a good laugh, a relieved sigh. That was my first big bicycle tour; we had enjoyed it very much, including the boat trip on the river. Except for the first day, the weather had been perfect also.

WE'RE GETTING MARRIED

We were engaged for two years; and on June 14, 1952, we got married. The evening before the wedding is *Polterabend. Polter* means lots of noise. Friends, neighbors, and relatives have saved old dishes for that night. They were thrown down at our door and burst into hundreds of pieces. It is supposed to bring good luck. The groom has to clean it all up with a broom later. All the ones that had thrown dishes at our door were invited into the house and got some cake. Neighbor's children usually take advantage of the situation and come back several times. Relatives and close friends stay longer. My friends put a wreath of white flowers in my hair. We celebrated till midnight, and slowly everyone went home.

In the morning, we had to go to city hall first, where a justice of the peace married us. That ceremony is demanded by law; we also had to bring two witnesses. I was wearing a new outfit that I had made for that special day. My hat was a *kuli* type, the latest hit. After the ceremony, the city presented us with a cookbook bound in linen, which I still have today and which I used often. The yellowed pages have wonderful recipes, older ones, the way Mom had cooked all those years. I certainly needed it then; except for baking, I had no experience at cooking meals. Mom had hired a cook for our special day; this way she had the time to enjoy the festivities too.

There was not enough money then to celebrate in a hotel. But our dinner was special and everyone enjoyed it.

The church wedding was at three in the afternoon. Walter's parents volunteered to pay for the taxi. The company sent two cars over: one was new and the other was an older model. While I changed into my wedding dress, the family was driven to the church. My in-law's turn to ride to church was in the old taxi. They didn't like it, and Mom came upstairs and complained. I told her that I didn't care, then we'd take the old car. But as we went downstairs, the newer car was awaiting us. Little white flower wreaths hung in the windows, which made it look festive, and everyone who saw it knew that a young married couple was in the car after or on the way to the church. No one thought to pick up the pastor; he had to ride to church with his bicycle and was a little late. My second disappointment came when I saw my sister's dress. It was a white dress with a green underskirt showing through the eyelet fabric. The bride was supposed to be the only one wearing white; it hurt my feelings. And the dress was made the same as mine. It really hurt a lot; Mom and Renate should have known better. It gave my special day a bitter taste. There seemed to be always this rivalry between my sister and me. Why? Why do this on my wedding day? What were they thinking? Were they not thinking at all? These little bits and pieces over the years make me want to go far away. I never had felt equally loved.

But I hate confrontations; my parents did enough of that. I kept quiet and hoped things would improve. My friend from work had made my dress—a white tulle with a baby blue underskirt. My dress had a little bolero to wear to cover the shoulders; Renate's dress also. My veil was attached to a little cap covered with white swan feathers, something new; usually the flowers were white, but mine were red roses. I had made Mom's dress, and Walter looked sharp in his black tuxedo. Our wedding ceremony was in the cathedral downtown. All the churches had been bombed during the war; and now, seven years after the war, they were only partly repaired. But we had a roof over our head where we were standing. We had trained ourselves not to see the ruins anymore, or we got used to seeing them; I don't remember. The paintings inside the cathedral were washed away by the rains. It was a place of beauty destroyed after nine hundred years. A place where emperors were buried along with an English princess. Their resting places had not been damaged. We had to pass them walking to the altar. The stony figures made me feel uneasy; they had died so long ago. After the ceremony, the taxi drove us to the photographer and then home after the pictures were taken. The rest of the guests were waiting at home. We had taken the furniture out of the living room to have enough room for everyone to sit down around several tables. Mom had time to enjoy the company, and finally, I could sit down and rest too. Later in the day, we had a cold supper. Several alcoholic beverages were served, and everyone had a good time. We did not have wedding cakes then like we have now. But lots of beautiful cakes were served. Several years later, Germany's brides had the same tiered cakes as we have here in the States.

The custom is that the bride's veil is taken off by her friends after midnight, and each one tears a piece out as a remembrance of the day. After that, the couple wears nightcaps. Mine was a lacy one, made by my friends. Walter's was a cotton one, pointed, with the tip falling over to one side. After a while, we tried to disappear discreetly. We thought we had been smart hiding my suitcase behind a door. Walter's father was watching; and as we tried to sneak out the door, my father-in-law stopped us and said, "Don't make babies, we want to go to the States first." I could only think that once we arrive in America, we could do what we wanted to do, finally! Dream on, Sigrid.

The taxi drove us to Walter's apartment. Before we could enter his room, we had to move a chest away, which blocked the door. This was also a custom. We had to eat a piece of bread with some salt; it meant we would always have food. When I undressed, I found a little bag with bread crumbs and salt sewn in the skirt of my dress. Also, two little baby dolls about one inch long—another custom to hope your marriage will be blessed with children.

I was kind of embarrassed when I got up in the morning; it was better to go right away on honeymoon. But money still mattered, and it was in short supply. We booked a trip to the Moselle valley, and we left three days later. Traben-Trarbach, where we stayed, is a picturesque town surrounded by vineyards. With every meal, people drink the Moselle wine. On the second day in town, we had a dance evening, and musical chairs were played. I won a bottle of wine, and so did the other couple sitting at our table. We started talking and drinking and learned that they were also going to New Jersey in the United States, the same as our destination. We spent a lot of time with them sightseeing and, of course, talking and dreaming about the future; we also exchanged our future addresses in the States. That one-week vacation passed pretty fast with a trip along the Moselle and Rhine Rivers and a bus trip to Trier to view the Roman ruins. Two years later, we met again in New Jersey; they had a little girl during the time we were separated. We are still friends today.

Back home, we prepared for Walter's trip to the United States. His Lionel train, which he got from his parents as a little boy, had to be packed securely. His father had played with it more than Walter, I was told. Those few weeks passed fast, and finally, we were on our way to Hamburg. The first night, we stayed with my friend Else, who had crossed the border with us so many years ago and who had two pretty little girls now. It was nice to renew our friendship and talk about old times. The next night, we stayed in a camp near the harbor where all the emigrants gathered for the embarkation the next morning. Walter crossed the ocean on the *Italia*, an Italian liner. He got last instructions from his father to enjoy the trip and to take his wedding ring off. I don't know who is worse, my father or his! As his ship left the harbor and the band played "Auf Wiedersehen," we stood there kind of lost. Then we found out that we could rent a boat and follow the ship for a while. We had to run to get a boat, but it was so little, only large enough for four people. As we got closer, Walter was not on deck anymore. I was glad to get back; the Elbe River had already very high waves, and our boat ride was a very choppy one. From there, we went to the railroad station, and the tears finally came. The enormity of our undertaking hit me like a sledgehammer; all of a sudden, I was scared. What awaited us over there? No family, no friends, another language, so many other languages spoken.

But the routine of everyday life helped; I was distracted during the day. One night a week, I took English lessons. They taught the Oxford English in Germany. After several weeks, I got a severe cold and needed sinus surgery. My hospital stay was only a week; the young doctor was really nice and attentive. I passed out three times during the surgery. Either it was too much sedation or the nurse pushed on the artery in my neck while she was holding my head up. The surgery was done with local anesthesia. I had to move my eyes so the doctor would not cut the muscles that controlled my eye movements. A piece of bone was cut out, and after that, my sinuses stayed open. The following day, two doctors came and checked my tummy; they prodded here and there. Then the question was asked, "Could you be pregnant?" My answer was, "No, my husband is in America." They thought that was very funny. The following week, I went back to work. Now it was about time to order the chest for my overseas voyage. A friend knew a carpenter who could make a large chest for me, big enough for me to pack all my belongings into. My friend Mara helped me pick it up from the carpenter when it was finished. Snow was on the ground, which was a blessing. It was easier to transport the chest home on a sled. We could not have managed it otherwise. It took us a whole hour to walk home, and then we had to carry and pull that chest up three flights of stairs. What a job, but we were young and strong. All my belongings fitted into the chest—my bed linens, comforters, towels, and dishes.

Walter wrote that he had a job with Westinghouse as a model maker, making two dollars an hour. I could exchange the two dollars for eight deutsche marks. I felt we were rich; I was getting more confident. He wrote that he was going to night school and to technical school to become acquainted with all the names of the tools and machines he had to work with. He lived in a boardinghouse with people he knew from years back when he still lived in the United States. The Thalheimers were an older couple who rented rooms to three men and one woman. They had emigrated from Germany years before too. Walter's father had moved to the States in 1922, came back to Germany later, married, and then moved back to Mahanoy City, where they had distant relatives from his mother's side. When Walter's grandfather died, he and his dad went to Germany for the funeral. It was still the Depression, and my father-in-law found work in Germany as an accountant, a job he had before he had immigrated to the United States. In Pennsylvania, he had worked in the coal mines, painted buses, sold books—jobs he had not really cared to do.

Letters came from Walter every week, one for his parents and one for me. He told me that it was not so easy, but his parents got a letter where everything was beautiful. At least he was honest with me; or did his parents make up a story? Walter applied for a visa for me; it was supposed to take five months before I could get it. I had to go to Hamburg for a medical checkup and to the American consulate. It took a whole day, and I barely made the train back home that night. Our checkup was very thorough. We had to stay in a line in groups of ten, naked. They checked us from top to bottom, in every nook and cranny—very embarrassing. I felt like a soldier, like a recruit lining up. At the embassy, the consul asked me questions, and I had to sign a paper in which I promised not to go on welfare when I arrived in the United States. Walter mailed a package for Christmas with sweets and clothing. Things looked different; I had to get used to that. I gave them all to a friend. Walter's father confronted me one night at suppertime that he would be in the States before me. I was puzzled and looked at him with a confused look. My answer was not a confused one though; I told him if that would happen, I would not go at all. He had not expected that answer. After I asked Walter what was going on, he told me not to worry; he would never get his father before me. But his father had tried; he had written to the family where his son was staying and had asked them to please influence his son that his father should come first. Finally, in January 1953, my visa and ticket arrived.

My friends gave me a going-away party. I got a pair of nylon stockings as a good-bye present. Pantyhose had not been invented then. The stockings were a brown shade with black seams in the back and borders around the heels in the back—something new, the latest style in stockings. One pair cost fifteen marks. We didn't touch them with our bare hands; we wore gloves when putting them on. Now, I thought, I was ready for America.

My friends came to the railroad station in the morning to see me off. Mom and Renate were coming with me. Bremerhaven was the port I was leaving from; it was on the mouth of the Weser River. My friends sang "Auf Wiedersehen" as the train left the station. And we waved till we were out of sight. The ship was the SS *United States*—a new ship, the largest and fastest on her second voyage. We looked around the ship and went to my cabin. And then the announcement came that all visitors had to leave the ship. A few more hugs and kisses, and both Mom and Renate left. I was staying on deck till we slowly left the dock. It took awhile before I saw them in the crowd of people. People shouted and waved as we slowly moved away from the dock. The musicians on deck were playing "Auf Wiedersehen," and Mom and Renate were waving till we couldn't see each other anymore. My eyes filled with tears, but they couldn't see that.

Le Havre was our first stop, where we got some more passengers. The English Channel was very choppy, so I went inside to my cabin. I was traveling tourist class. Another young woman and a mother with a small child were with me in my cabin. She liked to have my bed on the bottom so she could be closer to help her son if he needed her. It made sense, so I slept in the upper bunk. I unpacked my suitcase and went to the dining room; lunch would be served. I held back with my selection and wondered what it was I was ordering. English sounded different on the ship than in the classroom, and we had not discussed menus. We were told to complain if we didn't get good service. The ship company had to hire only union members, and not everyone was trained to be a good steward, but I had no problems with the one that had to take care of me. At night, we had several choices on what to do. I decided to go dancing; the musicians were good, but who wanted to dance with a married lady? Coke cost 1.50 marks in Germany. I gave the waiter 1.00 dollar and told him, "It's okay, no change." The people sitting next to me told me that a Coke was only 15 cents. No wonder they were so helpful and smiled at me all the time. The tip was very generous.

The next day, we stopped in South Hampton to take on more passengers. As we got into the Atlantic Ocean, the storm increased; the waves were as high as the ship. Slowly passengers got sick; people vomited. You had no control over it; it just came out of your mouth in a high curve. Stewards were busy cleaning up the mess all the time. It was hard to navigate the stairs with the ship going up and down. If the waves went down, you would start running; and if the waves went up, you would make tiny steps real fast. They had no stabilizers then as they have now. People did not leave the chairs on the upper decks; they felt safer sitting on the upper decks to look at the ocean. After breakfast, I felt the need for fresh air and went outside. I was glad that I was wearing slacks; it was pretty windy, and skirts would be a nuisance. They would fly way above my head. I had to lean into the wind as I was walking along one side of the ship. When I turned the corner, the other side was mayhem. Ropes were strung in all directions; I had to hold on for dear life. How could one side be relatively calm and the other have so much wind? I held on to the ropes with both hands and inched forward slowly to find a door to go inside. The wind was tearing on my clothes, and my arms were getting tired; all I could do was just hold on to the rope. A seaman was watching from the door, and when he saw my predicament, he came to my aid. Needless to say, I never went out again till the storm subsided.

My next supper selection was a disaster too. I saw vegetarian plate on the menu and believed I would get vegetables. The steward came with a beautifully arranged giant plate of all kinds of fish. We Germans love fish, smoked and otherwise. The steward saw my face and wanted to bring something else. But I saw many delicacies that I do know; so I ate what I liked. After that, I waited and saw what the others ordered at my table, and then I placed my selection. That night, out of the six hundred tourist-class passengers, only forty came to the dining room. Half the stewards leaned against the wall, their faces green. The next three days, I was mostly in my bed and ate sandwiches. After the meal, I threw up again. I never had ginger ale before, but after I tried it, I drank a lot of that; I enjoyed the taste. Our voyage took six days, one day longer than the previous one. I was glad when I could pack my suitcase and when I knew that tomorrow, we would arrive in New York. The night was a short one; with all the anticipation, I couldn't sleep much. At four in the morning, I could hear other cabin doors opening and closing. People were going on deck, and so did I. It was cold outside; the sea was calm, and the ship had slowed down.

We saw a dark stretch of land, and slowly, the lights came on in the houses, and we could see cars moving along the coastal highway. There were a few at first, but as it got lighter outside, the coastal traffic increased. After six days of heavy storms, the seas were calm, and a new life was in the distance. And then we passed the Statue of Liberty; it was a very emotional moment. Newcomers thought of all the people that had come before them on much smaller ships with all the hopes and dreams and expectations of a better life ahead. Skyscrapers were slowly lighting up; what a beautiful sight. The mouth of the Hudson River was gigantic, and I knew I would live on the other side in New Jersey. I didn't think that there was even one person without tears in their eyes. The ship glided slowly into our pier, and we passengers were directed to different exits. Debarking the ship went slowly, and then I heard talking and shouting only in English, and it was not the Oxford English that I learned; it was all accents combined, everyday slang, slurred speech. I couldn't understand anything, and worst of all, I could not see my husband anywhere. I just followed some people and stayed in line after them, and my eyes searched the crowds to try to find Walter.

And then I spotted him about forty yards away at another exit. I dropped everything and ran toward him. Dropping my bags in New York? Even then, it was a very risky thing to do. His friend was with him; he had a car. They ran back and got my smaller suitcase. I learned later why you can't leave anything alone on a pier in New York. The exit I had left on was first class, and Walter had waited at tourist class. Now we had to find my giant chest and go through customs. I could see it high above the ship in a net being lowered to the pier. It took several hours; I had to empty my whole chest completely. None of my dishes were broken. I had brought a dozen of everything—dinner dishes, coffee dishes, glassware, and crystal pudding dishes. Everything was whole. And then I had to repack. Was I too excited? Did I rush too much? When the chest reached us several days later, my pretty pudding dish was broken. But it was only one piece; after that long trip, I really can't complain.

Walter had brought a large bouquet of gladiolas for me. It took us one hour to drive to New Jersey. The Holland Tunnel was impressive, but I wasn't really very fond of tunnels. Thinking that there were masses of water above me made me feel nervous. We had walked under the Elbe tunnel in Hamburg before Walter had left, and I wanted to turn around then too. Walter's friend was surprised that I didn't make any comments about the skyscrapers. I had seen them in movies, in books, and on calendars; we had learned about the United States in school, so it was nothing new for me. When we arrived in Irvington, Walter's landlady had prepared a large turkey dinner and also invited her son with his family. The sweet potatoes were new for me, also the celery stalks. Everything else was familiar and tasted fantastic. Mrs. Thalheimer still cooked the German way. We stayed two more weeks at her house.

Walter had found an apartment, but he wanted me to choose the furniture. We started looking the next day. He had to go back to work and took me along in the bus so I would know which way to go the next day. His place of work was in Newark. The bus ride was five cents then. I just had to ride back and find my way. The next day, I made the trip by myself but in the afternoon, just before five. Getting closer to downtown, I thought the bus drove another way; and sure enough, the end of the ride was different from the day before. What to do now? Walter was nowhere in sight. I decided to just walk around the block; I should arrive back from where I started right? As I walked slowly around the block, I saw a frantic figure running toward me. He had forgotten that the evening bus took a slightly different route. *End good, all is good.*

Before we entered the large department store, Mr. Neubert, another friend from years back, saw us. "Let me call my wife," he said, "to tell her that I will be late. You can't purchase furniture by yourselves, I have to go with you." Why, why, somebody again who wanted to tell us what to do? I had thought I had escaped all the people that forced me to do what they wanted. After the phone call, he explained. We had to pay on credit, and we needed somebody to cosign. What a nice man to do that. I had thought that people would believe you when telling them that you would pay back in a timely fashion. When I saw the furniture, I had to suppress my tears. Everything was different, not at all what I had seen in the furniture stores in Germany. Over there, everything was modern; here, the furniture looked like antiques. The pictures I had in my head on how I wanted to furnish our apartment, I had to forget. Some dreams had to be buried.

Mr. Neubert suggested that we buy good quality so it would last a lifetime. We picked a mahogany suite and a kitchen table and four chairs. The kitchen set, I liked; the chrome chairs and table were something new. I loved those, light gray with red, my favorite color. We were now six hundred dollars in debt and had to pay it off in one year. When the furniture arrived, we were finally alone. The apartment was on the third floor; each room had slanted walls. Every time I do the dishes and store them, I bump my head on the ceiling walls since the storage place was so small. I could hang up about five garments in the clothes closet. The bathtub had a slanted wall too; you could only stand in there with your body bent over. But it was okay; in Germany, we would only get one room. Housing was still a serious problem when we left. The people we rented from and also the couple on the second floor were very nice. We had to pay fifty-five dollars' rent. At the time, it was hard to get an apartment when you were young. Landlords did not want to rent to couples that were young enough to get children.

I started night school too till Walter's parents came over. After I was four weeks in the country, a man came to my door with some papers and wanted some money. He said I owed them for shipping my large chest. I told him that I had a receipt to prove that I paid for the shipping charges. He left, and two days later, I read in the newspaper a warning that longshoremen were collecting an additional shipping fee from the new immigrants. I had met the first crook and did not fall for his scam. Ha-ha. In my English class, I met some German girls, and we spoke German before the teacher came into the class. She would always tell me, "Sigrid, speak English." It was so nice to have someone who spoke my mother tongue, who was from the old country, in the classroom. She did not understand how it feels when you are suddenly transplanted and hear only English.

Walter had to take the advanced class. Since I did not talk much in class, the teacher believed that I did not do the homework myself. She made me write it on the blackboard, and then I had to read it to the class. She realized that I could do it, but it was embarrassing for me. I did not like it that she did not trust me. My strong accent embarrassed me; that's why I avoided speaking English. In New York, New Jersey, or Pennsylvania, you hear lots of people talk with an accent; no one really notices. They have so many newcomers all the time. People are used to it, and if I said something wrong, they politely corrected me. Except my neighbors; they wanted me to sing and talk. Their little three-year-old daughter loved me. I talked to her in German, and she knew what I was saying. I didn't have enough to do in our small apartment and asked Patty if she wanted to come along for a walk. She nodded her head, but I told her that she needed a coat; it was cold outside. She told her mother to give her the coat. She understood what I was saying, and we went for a walk.

Walter and I and his friend went out a lot together. We saw all the sights in New York, visited the museums, experienced a different lifestyle. Going to the seashore was very special. I had not seen the ocean before, only from the ship. This was different—the smell, the sand, and the heat. We experienced a terrible sunburn. We were in love, and Walter brought home flowers every weekend. Visiting museums was always the first thing we did after moving. Walter's parents came eight months later. They wanted to travel first class, but Walter changed the tickets. We did not have the money first class would cost.

Here, I like to stop my story. A sad time in my life started, and Walter's parents are dead now. I feel there is no need to tell all the unpleasant things they did. My children know. Maybe if I had spoken up earlier like I wanted to, things would have been different; we will never know. Sometimes some people will never change. I am happy that I immigrated to the United States. It was not always easy to be so far away from my family. But we made it.

A Journey

War, destruction, finally peace,
Don't let it happen again.
Power-hungry politicians,
Speeches, promises—all false.
Speak up, get involved, educate.
Finally more food, work, living space,
Something new to plan for.
The urge to travel,
Sweden maybe, it's not too far.
The friend you meet says America.
Finally marriage—he follows his dream.
Waiting for visa, writing letters
And six months later, I'm on the ship.
A giant, the largest, the SS *United States.*
Five days to freedom?
What will it bring?
Stormy weather, seasickness.
And finally you see the Statue of Liberty.
In the early-morning dawn, all are on deck to view the sight.
The coast of the States in the morning light.
Your throat tightens, tears flow,
After the good-byes, a meek hello.
What will it be, this new land of the free?

America

Arrive in New York, go through customs
Unpack everything I own, my trunk, my suitcase
Understand nothing that is said
English sounds different in New York
Oxford English is what I learned in school
This is New York—here slang is cool
I repack the trunk, it's too large for the car
Everything is big in America
The highways, houses, cars, and trucks
Four weeks later, a knock on the door
It's the longshoreman, he wants more
More money for shipping the trunk, he said
My reply, I paid already on the dock
In the paper two days later I found out
I had the first crook in my house
Several tried to fleece the greenhorns that came
What a shame

Missing You

Why did I leave the country I loved?
Was it adventure that led me away?
The war I lived through?
The devastation of houses and land?
I miss my homeland as I get old.
The woods, the mountains,
The streams and hollows,
The parks to walk in.
When I go home it is not the same.
So many strangers walking the street.
Different languages spoken, new customs now.
When I go home I want things the same.
The same as always so many years ago.
I miss you, sister, you died too soon.
I miss you, Mom, gone is my home.
My homeland, my refuge, I feel so alone.

AFTERWORD

And now I like to thank everyone who touched my life in one way or another. This country has been good to me. The people I met over the past fifty-eight years have been loving and kind with their affections. Thanks to every one of you. May God bless you.

INDEX